Glenstone Field Guide

Published on the occasion of the opening of the Pavilions at Glenstone in 2018.

Editors: Emily Wei Rales, Anne Reeve, Fanna Gebreyesus
Text Editor: Claire Lehmann
Art Direction/Design: Aï Bihr
Graphic Design: Steven Wu
Illustrator: Jordan Awan
Printing: Spectragraphic in cooperation with Rolling Press
Published by: Glenstone Museum

First Edition: © 2018, Glenstone Museum, Potomac, Maryland

Every attempt has been made to identify and obtain permission from owners of copyrighted material included herein. Errors or omissions that are brought to our attention will be corrected in subsequent editions.

All rights reserved. No part of this publication may be reproduced or transmitted in any form or by any means, electronic or mechanical, including photocopy, recording, or any other information storage and retrieval system, otherwise without written permission from Glenstone Museum.

Glenstone Museum
12100 Glen Road
Potomac, Maryland 20854
www.glenstone.org

ISBN: 978-0-9998029-2-2
LCCN: 2018904960

Table of Contents

4	Contributors
7	Key
8	Map
11	Tips
13	Art
75	Architecture
93	Landscape
117	Index
119	Notes

Adam Greenspan (AG)
Landscape Architect

Alana Hill (AH)
Reporting and Applications Administrator

Alexandria Sayers (AS)
Curatorial Intern

Ali Nemerov (AN)
Assistant Curator

Amani Lewis (AL)
Guide

Anne Reeve (AR)
Associate Curator

Bill Lehan (BL)
Chief Engineer

Brian Patterson (BP)
Chef

Carly Davis (CD)
Assistant Librarian

Chris Ryan (CR)
Split-Rocker Specialist

Clive Jerram (CJ)
Building Engineer

Colleen Garibaldi (CG)
Guide

Elijah Majeski (EM)
Guide

Emily Benoff (EB)
Guide

Emily Grebenstein (EG)
Communications Manager

Emily Wei Rales (EWR)
Founder and Director

Eric Love (EL)
Landscape Superintendent

Eric Thornton (ET)
Guide

Fanna Gebreyesus (FG)
Editorial Assistant

Jamiee Shim (JSh)
Guide

Jason Hedges (JH)
Information Technology Manager

Jon Sander (JSa)
Aquatic Horticulturist

Karen Vidángos (KV)
Communications Coordinator

Kati Borchelt (KB)
Operations Coordinator

Kaylie Ngai (KN)
HR Coordinator

Laura Linton (LL)
Chief Administrative Officer

Contributors

Leigh Rollins (LR)
Guide

Margy Rodgers (MR)
Horticulturist

Gaby Mizes (GM)
Director of Registration

Martin Lotz (MLo)
Director of Facilities

Mary Beth Tsikalas (MBT)
Director of Finance and HR

Matt Partain (MP)
Deputy Superintendent of Grounds

Max Levin (MLe)
Guide

Michelle Clair (MC)
Visitor Experience Senior Manager

Mitchell P. Rales (MPR)
Founder

Natalya Rapundalo (NR)
Administrative Coordinator

Nora Severson Cafritz (NSC)
Manager of Curatorial Affairs

Paul Goldberger (PG)
Architectural Critic and Historian

Paul Tukey (PT)
Chief Sustainability Officer

Peter Ibenana (PI)
Community Outreach Coordinator

Rebecca Altermatt (RA)
Chief Archivist and Librarian

Samantha Halstead Santez (SHS)
Assistant Registrar

Samantha Owens (SOw)
Conservation Fellow

Samantha White (SW)
Guide

Sarah Elder (SE)
Guide

Steve Carrick (SC)
Director of Engineering and Maintenance

Steven O'Banion (SO)
Director of Conservation

Stockton Toler (ST)
Director of Visitor Experience

Tessa Brawley-Barker (TBB)
Librarian

Tim Butler (TB)
Head Preparator

Tim Curley (TCu)
Horticulturist

Tony Cerveny (TCe)
Chief Operating Officer

Tornike Gamziani (TG)
Security Officer

Thomas Phifer and Partners (TPP)
Architect

Tuong Huynh (TH)
IT Specialist

Valentina Nahon (VN)
Director of Design and Development

Key

| | **Subject** |
| Term | **(e.g., Artist's Name)** |

| | A short definition exploring an element of art, architecture, or landscape you may encounter, as described by a Glenstone associate or |
| Definition | collaborator. |

| Contributor | – Author Initials |

| | See Also: |
| Cross-Reference | Related Term (Page Number) |

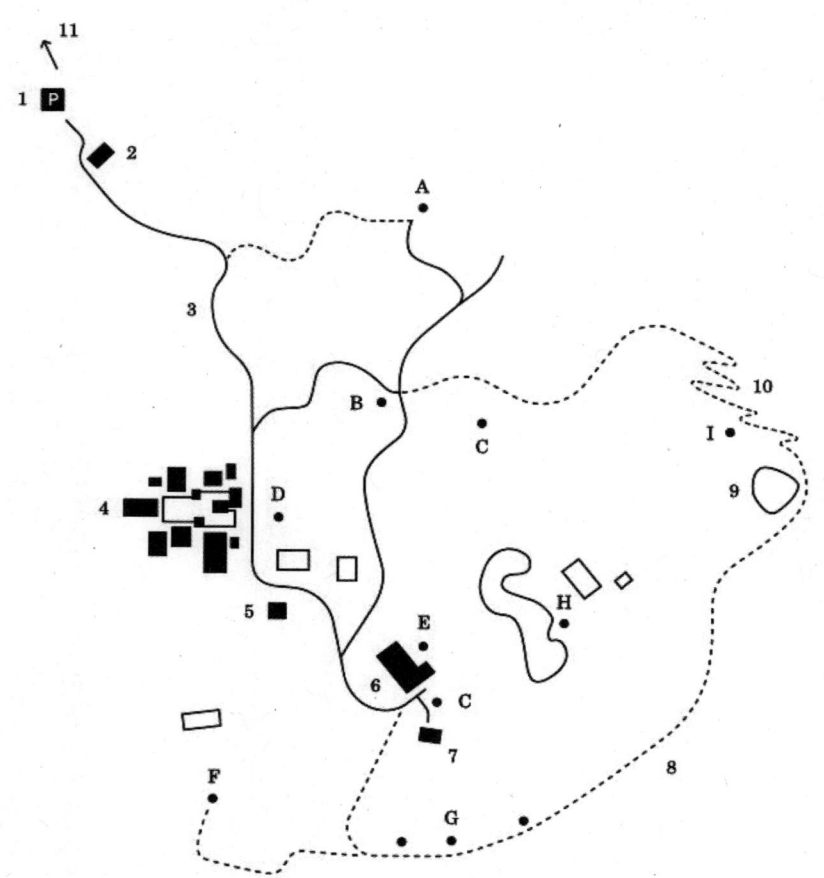

Map

1 Parking Groves
2 Arrival Hall
3 Main Path
4 The Pavilions
5 Café
6 The Gallery
7 Patio
8 Woodland Trail
9 Lily Pond
10 Boardwalk
11 Environmental Center

A Jeff Koons
B Tony Smith
C Richard Serra
D Michael Heizer
E Felix Gonzalez-Torres
F Janet Cardiff and George Bures Miller
G Andy Goldsworthy
H Ellsworth Kelly
I Robert Gober

Tips

1. We love art. We love our visitors. We love visitors who love art. That said, we ask that you refrain from touching the artworks (including the outdoor sculptures). This helps us preserve and protect this stuff we care so much about.

2. Any questions? Just ask any Glenstone guide or associate (wearing a silver bar pin) for assistance. We are here to help!

3. When you want to sketch or jot down a note, feel free to use a pencil to record thoughts about your Glenstone experience in the notes section at the back of this book (fun fact: the grid used for this section is the one Thomas Phifer and Partners used in the early stages of designing the Pavilions).

4. We don't allow photography indoors (we're hoping you use your eyes, not your viewfinder, to experience the art), but feel free to snap away in the landscape. We just ask that you watch the art, and your step, when taking any pictures—especially when it's selfie time!

5. There's a lot to explore outdoors at Glenstone, and we hope you explore it all. Wheelchairs are available on a first-come, first-served basis. Please note that the Woodland Trail covers varied terrain and is intended to be experienced on foot.

6. We practice Leave No Trace principles at Glenstone. Please be mindful of the delicate environments you traverse by disposing of your trash in one of the provided receptacles, staying on trails, and keeping wildlife wild. We ask that you leave your pet at home. Service animals are welcome.

7. Stop by the Café and Patio to rest, refresh, and take in views of the forest. The Café offers communal seating and a seasonal, farm-to-table menu. The Patio provides counter service and offers tea, coffee, baked goods, and other light fare to enjoy inside or alfresco.

8. Glenstone is a tobacco-free site.

9. AND . . . we'd love to hear from you! Please share any feedback about your experience with us at visit@glenstone.org, or tag any photos or musings with the hashtag #glenstonemuseum.

Art

We believe that art has the power to help us understand our history, expand our sense of curiosity about the world, empower creativity, and form meaningful connections with others. Our collection focuses principally on artworks made following World War II, with special attention to the great "disruptors," artists and artworks that have directly impacted how the story of art has been told in our time.

All artwork on view at Glenstone comes from the museum's permanent collection, and we aim to present these works in an unhurried and contemplative environment. Whenever possible we work closely with artists and their representatives to ensure the best possible presentation of their work. The following section contains information about the various artists, media, and movements that are currently on view.

Abstract Expressionism

This famed movement is associated with a group of New York artists who rose to great prominence in the 1940s and 1950s. Abstract Expressionists believed that artmaking was best served by total expressive freedom, unencumbered by premeditation or preconception. Their processes resulted in abstract imagery intended to represent the artist's interior self, such as the color-saturated canvases of Mark Rothko, the dynamic and frenzied drip paintings of Jackson Pollock, and the densely gestural canvases of Willem de Kooning.

—TBB

See Also:
de Kooning, Willem (32)
Kline, Franz (45)
Pollock, Jackson (56–57)
Rothko, Mark (64)

Abstraction

Abstraction is an artistic approach that resists figurative or representational methods in favor of an exploration of the fundamental elements of visual composition: form, line, color, and texture. At Glenstone, many examples of abstract artworks can be seen in the galleries, such as paintings by Clyfford Still, Rosemarie Trockel, and Gutai artists in the Room 2 installation, and Brice Marden's *Moss Sutra with the Seasons*, 2010–2015, in the Pavilions. In the exhibition *Louise Bourgeois: To Unravel a Torment* in the Gallery, sculptures such as *The Quartered One*, 1964–1965, and *Noir Veine*,1968, explore abstraction in three dimensions. Out of doors, visitors can encounter abstract artworks in the context of the landscape, such as Ellsworth Kelly's *Untitled*, 2005, across the Gallery pond; Richard Serra's *Contour 290*, 2004, in the meadow; and Tony Smith's *Smug*, 1973/2005.

—AN and MLe

See Also:
Abstract Expressionism (14–15)
Arte Neoconcreta (16)
Bourgeois, Louise (22–23)
Gutai (39)
Kelly, Ellsworth (44)
Marden, Brice (48)
Serra, Richard (65)
Smith, Tony (68)
Still, Clyfford (69)
Trockel, Rosemarie (70)

Abstract Expressionism

Appropriation Art

The term *appropriation art* encompasses a wide range of practices in which existing imagery or objects are "borrowed" and recontextualized to generate new meaning. Marcel Duchamp's recasting of the everyday object as art (e.g., a bicycle wheel) is an early example; decades later, artists like Andy Warhol and Robert Rauschenberg took imagery directly from popular media in order to create their art. Another famous practitioner is Elaine Sturtevant, who pushed appropriation even further by re-creating famous works by other artists (including Duchamp and Warhol). Artists working with appropriation continue to question ideas of creativity, originality, and authorship—questions that feel especially relevant in the media-saturated twenty-first-century world.

—EM

See Also:
Duchamp, Marcel (32)
Hammons, David (39)
Rauschenberg, Robert (60)
Readymade (62–63)
Warhol, Andy (72)

Arman

b. 1928, d. 2005. Arman was a French-born American sculptor sometimes associated with Nouveau Réalisme, a French movement that evolved in parallel with Pop art in the 1960s. Like his peers, Arman was influenced by Marcel Duchamp and Dada, and his work explored the use of ready-made objects as well as themes of repetition, mass production, commodification, waste, and destruction. Such themes are evident in the work on view in the Room 2 installation: *Home Sweet Home II*, 1960, a conglomeration of gas masks in a wooden box. Ominous and impactful, this work is an example of Arman's Accumulations, a long-standing series made using found objects arranged in wall-mounted boxes. The work's sweet title betrays its darker implications, evoking the realities of European wartime life and its material residue.

—KV

See Also:
Assemblage (18)
Klein, Yves (45)
Nouveau Réalisme (54)

Arte Neoconcreta

Arte Neoconcreta was a postwar Brazilian movement formed in response to the European Concrete art style of the 1950s, whose aesthetic rigidity Brazilian Neoconcreta artists felt could not fully express the human experience. Arte Neoconcreta artists—who worked in an abstract idiom, thereby evading censorship by a dictatorial political regime—were concerned with the political and social as well as the aesthetic. This new means of expression was revolutionary in its focus on art as experience and on the relationship between people and art. Several artists associated with this movement are on view in the Pavilions, including Lygia Clark, Lygia Pape, Hélio Oiticica, and Mira Schendel.

—SE

See Also:
Clark, Lygia (26)
Oiticica, Hélio (54)
Pape, Lygia (55)
Schendel, Mira (65)

Appropriation art

Arte Povera

Arte Povera, translated from Italian as "poor" or "impoverished" art, was an Italian movement originally founded in the late 1960s, employing unconventional processes and materials. Its name, coined by the Italian art critic Germano Celant, reflects the humble nature of the materials used by its artists, including rags, twigs, and dirt in addition to traditional elements such as oil, canvas, and marble. Working with these materials was in part a challenge to conventional art institutions and art markets, as works incorporating such ephemeral substances resist easy commodification. Certain artists associated with Arte Povera are still alive and making work in this vein, including Marisa Merz, whose *Untitled*, 1977, is on view in the Room 2 installation.

–SW

See Also:
Boetti, Alighiero e (20)
Merz, Marisa (50)
Postwar art (58)

Asawa, Ruth

b. 1926, d. 2013. American abstract sculptor Ruth Asawa began making art as a child, leaving marks in the sand with her feet while working on her family's farm in California. Later, Asawa would continue to draw even while forcibly resettled in various World War II internment camps for Japanese-Americans. Today, Asawa is best known for the three-dimensional use of line in her woven wire sculptures—intricate, organic forms like *Untitled* (S.531, Hanging Six Lobed, Two Continuous Interlocking Forms), 1950, one of three works by Asawa on view in the Room 2 installation. Asawa believed in the power of art to effect social change, and was a committed arts and education activist throughout her life.

–SW

See Also:
Abstraction (14)
Community (85)
Sculpture (65)

Assemblage

Assemblage is a three-dimensional medium that utilizes prefabricated or found materials in a format analogous to two-dimensional collage. Referring to both process and product, assemblage can be traced throughout various movements in Western art history, beginning with Cubism in the early 1900s. In using materials not typically associated with fine art, these unexpected amalgamations expand the accepted notion of sculpture. Examples of this tendency and practice are widely demonstrated in works in Glenstone's collection, such as Robert Rauschenberg's *Gold Standard*, 1964, and Yayoi Kusama's *Accumulation on Cabinet No. 1*, 1963, both on view in the Room 2 installation.

–SE

See Also:
Arman (16)
Collage (26)
Bourgeois, Louise (22–23)
Readymade (62–63)

Avant-Garde

Coined in the nineteenth century, the term *avant-garde* originates from the French phrase for "vanguard" and has come to refer to art and artists at the forefront of innovation. Avant-garde art is ahead of its time, marching toward the unknown, daring the rest to follow. Whether fueled by political, historical, philosophical, aesthetic, or even personal motivations, avant-garde art challenges established standards through radical experimentation, questioning what seems unquestionable, and changing history along the way.

–EM

See Also:
Abstract Expressionism (14–15)
Arte Povera (18)
Exhibition (34)
Fluxus (34)
Gutai (39)

Baer, Jo

b. 1929. Born in Seattle, Jo Baer is a painter especially known for her Minimalist works from the 1960s and 1970s. These works are concerned with how boundaries and borders influence visual perception, as evidenced in *Untitled (Wraparound Triptych–Blue, Green, Lavender)*, 1969, on view in the Room 2 installation. This three-panel painting subtly reorients the viewer's perspective, using attenuated bands of color to pull focus from the front and center of the canvas to its sides—a gesture that emphasizes the three-dimensionality of the object and its relationship to the wall. Baer's practice later developed into what she now calls "radical figuration," which fuses symbols, images, and words into nonnarrative compositions.

–RA

See Also:
Abstraction (14)
Minimal art (50)
Painting (55)

Basquiat, Jean-Michel

b. 1960, d. 1988. American painter Jean-Michel Basquiat began his career as a musician and graffiti artist in his native New York. Born to parents of Haitian and Puerto Rican descent, Basquiat rose to prominence in the 1980s, rapidly shifting from spray-painting buildings as part of the artist duo SAMO to selling his paintings in esteemed SoHo galleries. An autodidact who easily crossed artistic boundaries, Basquiat drew on his pluralist heritage and his experiences of racism, recasting episodes from his past into canvases featuring novel arrangements of text, abstraction, and stylized figures. His work *Frogmen*, 1983, a six-panel mixed-media painting, is on view in the Room 2 installation.

–EG

See Also:
Collage (26)
Haring, Keith (39)
Warhol, Andy (72)

Benglis, Lynda

b. 1941. In the 1960s American sculptor Lynda Benglis developed a practice in direct reaction to the formalism—and, some would argue, the masculinity—of prevailing Minimalist trends. Employing unconventional materials such as wax, polyurethane, latex, and resin, Benglis emphasized process, allowing materials to dictate an artwork's final shape and form. The cast-aluminum work *WING*, 1970, on view in the Room 2 installation, exemplifies Benglis's innovative "pour" technique, which she developed and refined in the late 1960s. *WING* hangs off the wall like a painting; however, the amorphous metal extends out from the wall into three-dimensional space. Benglis's work often defies categorization, blurring the line between traditional painting and sculpture.

–NSC

See Also:
Post-Minimal art (58)
Process art (59)
Sculpture (65)

Beuys, Joseph

b. 1921, d. 1986. Joseph Beuys is widely recognized as one of the most significant postwar artists of the twentieth century. Beuys believed that "ideas are communicated through men," and as a self-described "social sculptor," his oeuvre primarily consisted of performance works, documentary photography, and "multiples," a range of modestly sized and affordable artifacts related to his broader practice. He embedded materials with deep metaphorical meanings, often related to his compelling, if implausible, autobiography: Beuys maintained that he had been saved from a plane crash in the Mongolian mountains by Tartar tribesman following World War II, men who healed him by wrapping him in fat and felt. This self-mythologizing contributed strongly to Beuys's quasi-shamanic persona in the art world, and his lasting influence on the history of art.

–LR

See Also:
Avant-garde (19)
Postwar art (58)

Boetti, Alighiero e

b. 1940, d. 1994. Italian artist Alighiero e Boetti created a lastingly radical body of work in a comparatively short lifetime. Boetti was especially interested in the concept of "twinning," or communicating between two selves (he added the *e*—"and"—between his first and last names in 1968 to suggest this plurality). Involved early on with the Arte Povera movement, Boetti distanced himself after 1972, and is now well known for his series of embroidered world maps made by commissioned Afghan artisans who fabricated the works according to his instructions. Boetti's maps engage differing cultures and aesthetics to create a unified object; one such work, *Mappa*, 1971–1972, is on view in the Room 2 installation, along with the artist's sculpture *Cubo*, 1968.

–JSh

See Also:
Arte Povera (18)
Conceptual art (28–29)
Postwar art (58)

Beuys, Joseph

Bontecou, Lee

b. 1931. American artist Lee Bontecou has a wide range of influences, including airplanes, politics, nature, and the body; her work stands at the crossroads of abstraction and figuration, the organic and mechanical, and the social and personal. Pushing the boundaries between sculpture and painting, *Untitled*, 1962, on view in the Room 2 installation, exemplifies these collective explorations: the work seems to extend from the wall into three-dimensional space while simultaneously recoiling into itself with three "black holes." Viewers have drawn connections between such works and the 1960s cultural and political preoccupation with the cosmos, space travel, and the race to moon.

—JSh

See Also:
Hesse, Eva (40–41)
Benglis, Lynda (20)
Postwar art (58)
Sculpture (65)

Bourgeois, Louise

b. 1911, d. 2010. Celebrated for her singular contributions to the fields of sculpture, drawing, painting, printmaking, installation, and writing, French-born American artist Louise Bourgeois's explorations of the human condition originate from her own lived experience. Psychologically, emotionally, and often sexually charged, Bourgeois's works intermingle the abstract and the corporeal to striking effect. *Louise Bourgeois: To Unravel a Torment*, on view in the Gallery, is the first exhibition of the artist's work at Glenstone and features nearly thirty major works from the collection, including examples of her early Personages, large hanging sculptures, suites of drawings and prints, textile works, and her immersive Cells.

—AN

See Also:
Assemblage (18)
Installation (42)
Printmaking (59)
Sculpture (65)

Broodthaers, Marcel

b. 1924, d. 1976. In 1964, Belgian-born poet Marcel Broodthaers declared himself a visual artist by exhibiting a sculpture of unsold copies of his book *Pense-Bête* (Memory Aid) embedded in plaster—a tongue-in-cheek gesture of "implanting" meaning into sculpture. Broodthaers's critical inquiry into the role of art and art institutions was a lasting concern, most famously enacted in his late 1960s project *Musée d'Art Moderne, Département des Aigles* (Museum of Modern Art, Department of Eagles)—a simulacrum of the traditional modern art museum, but without a collection or permanent site. Over the course of his short career, Broodthaers produced works distinguished by playful juxtaposition of quotidian objects and subversion of language. *Ovale d'oeufs 1234567* (Oval of Eggs 1234567), 1965, on view in the Room 2 installation, consists of dozens of eggshells—a popular motif in his oeuvre—with numerals inscribed on their surfaces.

—EB

Bourgeois, Louise

Calder, Alexander

b. 1898, d. 1976. American artist Alexander Calder first began making work as a child, influenced by his mother, father, and grandfather—all of whom were artists. Calder's proclivity towards building objects led to a lifelong interest in kinetics, and he acquired a degree in mechanical engineering before turning his full attention to art. By the late 1920s he was working as an artist in New York City, and around 1930 he began shifting from representational work to abstraction, prompted in part by his friendship with artist Piet Mondrian. Today Calder is widely recognized for his mechanized artworks and for pioneering a type of suspended kinetic sculpture that Marcel Duchamp famously dubbed "mobiles." *Baby Flat Top*, 1946, on view in the Room 2 installation, showcases Calder's unique marriage of engineering and abstraction.

—CD

See Also:
Abstraction (14)
Modern art (52–53)
Sculpture (65)
Tinguely, Jean (70)

Camargo, Sergio

b. 1930, d. 1990. Associated with the Brazilian Arte Neoconcreta movement, sculptor Sergio Camargo is especially known for his experimentation with sculptural reliefs. Extensive travel and an extended stay in Paris prompted Camargo's eventual fusion of Brazilian and European traditions; his meticulous assemblies of cuboid and cylindrical forms are made of wood, terra-cotta, stone, or marble, and typically supported on a white monochrome base. These forms respond to the organic interactions between shadow and light. Camargo believed that his materials would speak for themselves, once saying of his works that "they are only what they know how to be"—indicating that his abstract forms were driven by a working method that relied heavily on intuition.

Camargo's *Relief no. 259*, 1970, is on view in the Room 2 installation.

—EB

See Also:
Abstraction (14)
Arte Neoconcreta (16)
Clark, Lygia (26)
Oiticica, Hélio (54)
Schendel, Mira (65)

Calder, Alexander

Cardiff, Janet and George Bures Miller

Janet Cardiff, b. 1957. George Bures Miller, b. 1960. The Canadian-born collaborators are groundbreaking artists who utilize sound in their work. Believing that sound has the unique ability to "bypass your intellect . . . [to] go inside of you in a way that nothing else can," the duo draws from history, memory, and dreams, incorporating music, voices, quotidian noises, and jarring sounds to create multisensory artworks. Their outdoor installation *FOREST (for a thousand years . . .)*, 2012, is located along a secluded path in a forest clearing behind the Gallery. The work imagines what a forest might have heard over the course of a millennium, using Ambisonic technology and multiple speakers to create a "dome" of sound. *FOREST* creates an immersive experience, forging sound into a discrete space.

–LR

See Also:
Forest bathing (103)
Sound art (68)
Time-based media (69)
Woodlands (116)

Clark, Lygia

b. 1920, d. 1988. Lygia Clark was a pioneering Brazilian artist who cofounded the movement known as Arte Neoconcreta. Clark worked in many media and was committed to making art for the everyday person rather than only the elite. She was especially intrigued by the relationship between her art and its viewers, and made many works whose express purpose was for direct, tactile interaction. *Espaço Modulado 3*, 1959, is on view in the Room 2 installation.

–SOw

See Also:
Abstraction (14)
Arte Neoconcreta (16)
Oiticica, Hélio (54)
Pape, Lygia (55)

Collage

The term *collage* derives from the French word coller, meaning to paste or glue, and refers to the process—and end product—of adhering paper to a surface. Originating in the early twentieth century, collage techniques became popular with avant-garde artists who repurposed text and imagery, often newspapers and photographs, into their works. Removed from their original contexts, these extracts gain new meaning, as do the overall artworks of which they become a part. In the years since the term initially emerged, it has come to describe nearly any two-dimensional material incorporated within a larger work. Robert Rauschenberg's *Gold Standard*, 1964, on view in the Room 2 installation, incorporates elements of collage: various printed reproductions are adhered to a folding Japanese screen.

–FG

See Also:
Basquiat, Jean-Michel (19)
Mosaiculture (104)
Postmodern art (58)
Rauschenberg, Robert (60)

Cardiff, Janet and George Bures Miller

Collection

At Glenstone the "collection" refers to the totality of the museum's acquired artworks, including paintings, sculptures, works on paper, photography, videos, and time-based media. Some of these works are on view at Glenstone, others are in storage, and many are regularly loaned to other institutions for special exhibitions. The collection is thus a dynamic entity, constantly expanding and circulating. While Glenstone's collection contains a vast array of artistic ideas and forms of expression in works produced over the course of the past century, it is anchored by a commitment to quality, and by a desire to share these artworks, free of charge, with visitors.

–GM and MBT

See Also:
Avant-garde (19)
Commission (28)
Contemporary art (30)
Modern art (52–53)
Postwar art (58)

Commission

When collecting contemporary art, patrons or institutions might, on occasion, invite an artist to create a work that may then be acquired for the institution's collection. An artwork conceived in this way is known as a commission, and although its form may change during its making, typically its context is determined in advance. Works commissioned with a particular setting in mind at Glenstone include Richard Serra's *Contour 290*, 2004, and Andy Goldsworthy's *Clay Houses (Boulder-Room-Holes)*, 2007. In both cases, the artists sited their own outdoor sculptures in consultation with architects, structural engineers, and landscape designers. In the case of Brice Marden's multipanel painting *Moss Sutra with the Seasons*, 2010–2015, on view in the Pavilions, the process unfolded in reverse: the size, scale, and lighting scheme of the room were fixed only after Marden decided on the proportions and dimensions of his canvases.

–EWR

See Also:
Goldsworthy, Andy (36–37)
Marden, Brice (48)

Conceptual Art

Conceptual art rose to prominence in the 1960s as artists began using text, ready-made objects, performance, video, and other materials in ways that emphasized art as a practice of ideas. Sol LeWitt wrote a foundational essay in 1967 that defines the movement succinctly: "The idea or concept is the most important aspect of the work . . . the idea becomes a machine that makes the art." The original exhibition of the readymade *Fountain*, 1917/1964, by Marcel Duchamp (also now on view in the Room 2 installation), is considered a pioneering example of this way of thinking, challenging notions of traditional sculpture and the role of artistic creativity itself.

–MLe

See Also:
Cardiff, Janet and George Bures Miller (26–27)
Kruger, Barbara (46)
LeWitt, Sol (48)
Weiner, Lawrence (72–73)

Conceptual art

Conservation

Conservation is practiced across many disciplines, including art and architecture as well as landscape. It can be described comprehensively as a practice that includes careful examination, development of acceptable treatment, and implementation of proper preventive care with extensive documentation in order to contribute to the preservation of material culture. At Glenstone, conservation is an ongoing practice with a diverse range of activities that might include anything from inspections of dust on the yarn of a Fred Sandback artwork to symposia on paint composition used in outdoor sculpture to researching the ideal chemical balance of water used for cleaning and irrigation. Contemporary art conservation has expanded beyond the preservation of historic monuments to include working in conjunction with the artist while they are developing or installing their work. George L. Stout, a pioneering figure in the modern field of conservation, described the collaboration of art historians, scientists, and conservators as "the three-legged stool" that supports contemporary museum conservation.

—SO

See Also:
Climate control (76)
Collection (28)
Drawing (32–33)
Painting (55)
Reforesetation (105)
Sculpture (65)
Shade (83)
Stream restoration (108)
Sustainability (71)

Contemporary Art

Broad, ambiguous, and nearly impossible to categorize, the term *contemporary art* usually refers to art that is made in the present day. Art historically, contemporary art can also be used to describe works made beginning in the latter part of the twentieth century, following modernism, when narratives became less linear and developed a sharper focus on conceptualization and process. This designation often dovetails with "postwar art" as a descriptor for the artistic movements that brewed after World War II; the earliest exemplars of contemporary art generally have their origins in the 1960s (such as Pop art, Minimalism, and Conceptualism), while "postwar art" may also encompass movements dating from the 1940s, such as Abstract Expressionism. Today, contemporary art reflects an unprecedented plurality of voices, issues, politics, identities, and aesthetics—the art of our time.

—FG

See Also:
Collection (28)
Exhibition (34)

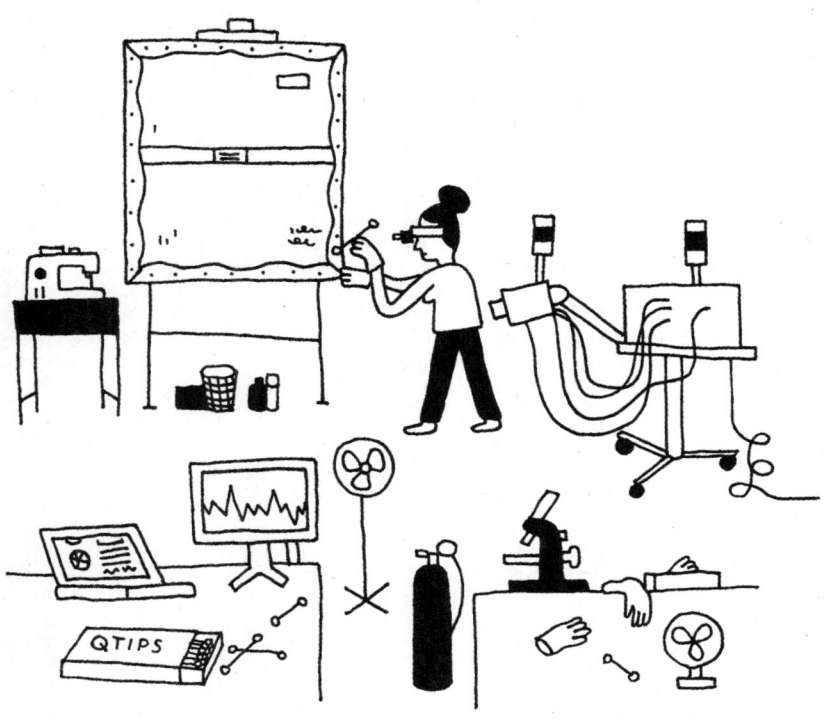

Conservation

de Kooning, Willem

b. 1904, d. 1997. Pioneering artist Willem de Kooning was born in Rotterdam and came to the United States in 1926 as a stowaway on a ship. He eventually moved to New York City and remained on the East Coast throughout his life, becoming an integral figure in the now-storied art scene of the day. Long revered as a founder of Abstract Expressionism, de Kooning initially trained as a commercial artist, working as a painter for the Works Project Administration Federal Art Project in the 1930s. His personal work boldly hybridizes abstraction and figuration; he is especially well-known for his provocative depictions of women and a dynamic use of color. An early and exemplary work, *January 1st*, 1956, is on view in the Room 2 installation.

–RA

See Also:
Abstract Expressionism (14–15)
Avant-garde (19)
Painting (55)

Drawing

From crayon scribbles to scientific renderings of nature, the act of drawing embraces countless materials and methods. Traditionally defined by the inscription of lines on a surface, most commonly graphite on paper, drawing was historically used—at least within the most recent millennium—primarily as a preparatory vehicle for paintings and architectural designs. However, many artists have since expanded the practice to encompass a myriad of tools and processes. Various works on view at Glenstone might be considered to utilize drawing, such as the pencil grid lines peeking through the surface of Agnes Martin's *Pilgrimage*, 1966; or the evocative inked figuration of Louise Bourgeois's *Ste. Sébastienne*, 1998.

–CG

See Also:
Bourgeois, Louise (22–23)
Haring, Keith (39)
Martin, Agnes (50–51)
Schendel, Mira (65)

Duchamp, Marcel

b. 1887, d. 1968. It is difficult to overstate the impact of French-born artist, writer, critic, and thinker Marcel Duchamp on the history of twentieth- and twenty-first-century art. While his list of artistic accomplishments is long and varied, he is especially known for a particular gesture first performed in 1914, when he took a mass-produced bottle rack and declared it art. This seemingly simple act—proposing that a shift in context was enough to take something ordinary and transform it into art—broke with centuries of tradition and set the stage for many of the significant artistic innovations of the past century. Two of Duchamp's most iconic "readymades," as he called them, are on view in the Room 2 installation—*Roue de Bicyclette*, 1913/1964, and *Fountain*, 1917/1964, which caused a scandal when Duchamp submitted it to the Salon des Indépendants in Paris in 1917.

–PI

See Also:
Conceptual art (28–29)
Modern art (52–53)
Readymade (62–63)

Drawing

Exhibition

At the core of Glenstone's mission is a commitment to organizing exhibitions that chart significant historical shifts in the perception and understanding of the art of our time. Selected exclusively from Glenstone's collection, temporary exhibitions rotate annually in the Gallery and Room 2 in the Pavilions. Past exhibitions include *The Inaugural Exhibition* (2006–2009), *If we could imagine* (2009–2011), *No Substitute* (2011–2013), *Peter Fischli David Weiss* (2013–2014), *Fred Sandback: Light, Space, Facts* (2015–2016), and *Roni Horn* (2017–2018). *Louise Bourgeois: To Unravel a Torment* is currently on view in the Gallery.

–AN

See Also:
Avant-garde (19)
Contemporary art (30)
Postwar art (58)

Flavin, Dan

b. 1933, d. 1996. American artist Dan Flavin began using his most iconic medium—fluorescent tubes—in the early 1960s. *a primary picture*, 1964, on view in the Room 2 installation, uses five fixtures and lamps to cast the primary colors of red, blue, and yellow. The off-the-shelf tubes are arranged in a simple rectangular shape, mimicking the composition of a traditional painting. As manufacturers phase out production of older lighting technologies in favor of LEDs, conservators of Flavin's work have begun stockpiling the tubes for future installations. Today the work serves as a demonstration of Flavin's singular achievement in generating new ways of viewing light, space, and art.

–TB

See Also:
Installation (42)
Light (82–83)
Minimal art (50)
Sculpture (65)

Fluxus

Founded by Lithuanian-American artist George Maciunas in the 1960s, the Fluxus movement united an international and interdisciplinary group of avant-garde artists, composers, designers, architects, mathematicians, philosophers, and poets. Working against the perceived elitism of "high art," the group was devoted to a total integration of art and life, and focused on creating multidisciplinary works composed from everyday materials and experiences. These works often include events that ask viewers to become participants in the process of creating the piece.

–AN

See Also:
Avant-garde (19)

Direct Engagement

We believe that the best way to experience art, architecture, and nature is in person, and with minimal intervention. Visits to Glenstone are intentionally designed to be open-ended and analog: there are no digital apps, audio guides, or touch screens here. The absence of didactic wall texts encourages you to generate your own interpretations about the works you encounter. Since visitors seek different levels of engagement and interests vary widely, guides (in gray uniforms with horizontal bar pins) are stationed throughout the campus to answer questions, discuss ideas, and offer general assistance as needed. You can also consult this book as an index on all things Glenstone.

—EWR and MPR

Giacometti, Alberto

b. 1901, d. 1966. Swiss artist Alberto Giacometti is best known for hyperelongated sculptures of the human form—the male figures generally in motion, the female figures upright and still. Many have described these works as physical embodiments of a postwar existential crisis, yet Giacometti was himself especially interested in the idea of perception. He spoke of trying to capture an interpretation of how things appear to us—rather than how they actually are—and his figures can seem as though compressed by the space around them, or as if always at a distance, impossible to fully grasp. *Man Pointing*, 1947, on view in the Room 2 installation, was made during a single frenzied nighttime work session and first shown in a 1948 exhibition at the Pierre Matisse Gallery in New York.

–EB

See Also:
Modern art (52–53)
Postwar art (58)
Sculpture (65)

Gober, Robert

b. 1954. American artist Robert Gober makes sculptural facsimiles of everyday objects that conjure complex associations, from the poetic to the political. *Untitled*, 1992, located in the Pavilions, features a dark corridor-like space that surrounds an interior room, in which a 360-degree painted mural of a forest provides a backdrop for a series of wall-mounted sinks, whose taps are flowing with a constant stream of water. Gober's replicas of boxes of rat bait; bound stacks of newspapers, some featuring a black-and-white image of the artist dressed in a wedding gown; and barred prison windows, which reveal a gentle blue sky beyond, round out the assortment of ambiguous symbols in this interior habitat. The artist's outdoor sculpture *Two Partially Buried Sinks*, 1986–1987, can also be seen nestled among the trees off of the Glenstone Boardwalk, adjacent to the Lily Pond.

–EM

See Also:
Pond (104)
Sculpture (65)
Soil (105–106)
Woodlands (116)

Goldsworthy, Andy

b. 1956. British sculptor Andy Goldsworthy sometimes creates art so ephemeral it lasts mere hours, using materials such as sheets of ice, fallen leaves, or twigs balanced precariously atop one another. Other works are more durable, like Glenstone's outdoor sculpture *Clay Houses (Boulder-Room-Holes)*, 2007, located in the woodlands clearing behind the Gallery and near the Greenbriar Branch stream. Built using locally quarried Carderock stone, this three-part work also utilizes clay excavated on the property. Goldsworthy's site-specific works are frequently in dialogue with—and often nearly camouflaged into—their environments, and encourage a sense of discovery and surprise for the viewer. Using humble materials to engage with themes such as place, nature, history, memory, and time, Goldsworthy's sculptures can feel as if they are delivering secrets from nature.

–MC

See Also:
Carderock (86)
Site-specific (66)
Soil (105–106)

Goldsworthy, Andy

Gonzalez-Torres, Felix

b. 1957. d. 1996. Cuban-American artist Felix Gonzalez-Torres challenged notions of audience engagement, believing that a viewer's interpretation completed his art. He also highlighted institutional responsibility by leaving certain elements of his works' fabrication open-ended, to be determined by the exhibitor. In the case of the outdoor sculpture "*Untitled*", 1992–1995, on view outside the Gallery, Gonzalez-Torres did not specify what material should be used. When the work was realized posthumously in 2007, Carrara marble was chosen because of its origin in Italy, where the piece was first shown, uniting a material more commonly associated with Classical statuary with the artist's Minimalist vocabulary. The twin round pools, each holding three hundred gallons of water and weighing over seven tons, form a figure eight, an often-repeated Gonzalez-Torres motif symbolizing togetherness and harmony.

—JSh

See Also:
Conceptual art (28–29)
Gallery, the (78)
Sculpture (65)
Stone (86–88)

Gorky, Arshile

b. 1904, d. 1948. Born as Vostanik Manoug Adoian, Arshile Gorky fled the Armenian genocide in 1915 and arrived in the United States in 1920. Reinventing himself as an artist, Gorky took a number of painting lessons in Boston and New York, and his notable early works include painted interpretations of a childhood photograph picturing the artist and his mother. Throughout the 1940s, Gorky found inspiration in pastoral Hamilton, Virginia, where he interpreted his surroundings in a unique visual language. *Drawing*, 1943, on view in the Room 2 installation, exemplifies how his emotive impressions are captured through vibrant fields of color; lines dance across the canvas, evoking the energy of an animated, verdant landscape.

—EM

See Also:
Abstract Expressionism (14–15)
de Kooning, Willem (32)
Painting (55)
Pollock, Jackson (56–57)
Postwar art (58)

Gutai

Visionary Japanese artist Jiro Yoshihara founded the Gutai art collective in 1954 and encouraged its members to create artworks unlike any that they had seen or experienced before. The resulting works often combined painting, performance, and interactive installation environments. The word *gutai*, which translates as "concreteness," embodies one of the movement's central tenets: to physically engage with novel materials in innovative ways. Indeed, in the Gutai manifesto, Yoshihara stated, "We have decided to pursue enthusiastically the possibilities of pure creativity. We believe that by merging human qualities and material properties, we can concretely comprehend abstract space." Artists associated with this movement include Akira Kanayama, Sadamasa Motonaga, Kazuo Shiraga, Shozo Shimamoto, Atsuko Tanaka, and Toshio Yoshida.

–AN

See Also:
Avant-garde (19)
Exhibition (34)

Hammons, David

b. 1943. American artist David Hammons is best known for reframing highly charged political and cultural symbols to address the experiences of African American citizens and communities, often with pointed humor. Hammons employs different mediums and draws from multiple influences, as evidenced in *How Ya Like Me Now?*, 1988, on view in the Room 2 installation. This large-scale portrait—painted on sheets of tin—was originally commissioned by the Washington Project for the Arts, and depicts the Reverend Jesse Jackson as a blond-haired, blue-eyed man. Viewers took issue with this portrayal, and *How Ya Like Me Now?* was vandalized when first installed publicly in downtown Washington, DC. Hammons subsequently decided to absorb the vandals' markings as part of the finished work, reframing the installation to include a stanchion of sledgehammers (the tool used to strike the piece) and an American flag as part of its display.

–TB

Haring, Keith

b. 1958, d. 1990. Influenced by his cartoonist father and 1970s popular culture, American artist Keith Haring began making art at a young age. Moving from Pennsylvania to New York in the 1980s proved incredibly influential to his work; soon after he arrived in the city Haring was living and working alongside fellow graffiti artists Jean-Michel Basquiat and Kenny Scharf. He developed a highly distinctive style of cartoon-like icons, including dancing figures, an infant emitting rays of light (his "radiant child"), barking dogs, and hearts. This singular visual language can be seen in his work *Untitled*, 10/22/1988, on view in the Room 2 installation. Haring also used art as a tool for activism, producing over fifty public artworks both in New York and abroad, and utilizing his increasing fame and influence to support humanitarian causes. Prior to his death at age thirty-one, Haring established the Keith Haring Foundation, which continues to support AIDs-related educational initiatives.

–CD

Heizer, Michael

b. 1944. American artist Michael Heizer uses earth as a medium to challenge the tradition of art as a salable object. Influenced by the ceremonial structures of ancient civilizations, his often-monumental work balances colossal scale and conceptual rigor, and made him a pioneer of Land art in the late 1960s. Two of Heizer's weathering-steel sculptures, on view in and outside the Pavilions, formally employ negative space and unseen force. In *Compression Line*, 1968/2016, tons of carefully compacted soil push against a large below-ground concave metal structure, forcing the two sides to meet at a common midpoint and creating a recessed geometric hollow in the landscape. In contrast, *Collapse*, 1967/2016, seems almost haphazardly arranged: massive metal beams—up to forty-two feet long—are strewn within a sunken steel cube, like discarded construction materials.

–SE

See Also:
Argillite (86)
Pavilions, the (83)
Sculpture (65)

Hesse, Eva

b. 1936, d. 1970. The German-born, New York–based artist Eva Hesse remains one of the most significant, singular, and influential artists of the postwar period. Often associated with her post-Minimalist—and predominantly male—peers, Hesse employed a variety of sculptural materials—resin, fiberglass, rope, rubber tubing—to create organic forms charged with psychological and bodily presence. Three works by the artist are on view in the Room 2 installation: *Several*, 1965; *Constant*, 1967; and *Sans II*, 1968.

–AS

See Also:
Abstraction (14)
Assemblage (18)
Post-Minimal art (58)
Sculpture (65)

Horn, Roni

b. 1955. For more than forty years, American artist Roni Horn has been creating a diverse oeuvre that spans drawing, sculpture, photography, installation, and books. Exploring wide-ranging topics, including human identity, ecology, landscape, weather, and language, Horn's work intermingles material and context, complicating relationships between object, subject, and viewer in the process. On view in the Passage in the Pavilions is *Water Double, v. 3*, 2013–2015, two of the largest solid cast-glass cylinders that the artist has created. One black and one translucent, these forms conceptually reflect on the dualities that Horn often explores in her work, while also literally incorporating the surrounding environment onto their surfaces.

–AN

See Also:
Glass (80)
Pavilions, the (83)
Post-Minimal art (58)
Sculpture (65)

Hesse, Eva

Installation

Installation is a term with multiple meanings in the context of art. It can refer to the work of preparing an artwork for exhibition, a process that can involve a range of specialists, including curators, conservators, registrars, preparators, and art handlers. The final product, i.e., artwork in situ, may also be considered an *installation*, as with Room 2 in the Pavilions, which includes iconic works from a broad spectrum of twentieth-century movements, such as Abstract Expressionism, Gutai, Brazilian modernism, Minimalism, and beyond. The term can also describe a type of artwork: the immersive work *Untitled*, 1992, by Robert Gober on view in the Pavilions, can be thought of as installation art, in which a work's disparate elements and objects are unified within a carefully considered environment that has been developed as an intentional part of the work's overall concept and display.

–AR and SO

Johns, Jasper

b. 1930. American painter, sculptor, and printmaker Jasper Johns creates works that, despite being centered around identifiable cultural signifiers, reject the possibility of being reduced to set meanings or interpretations. Influenced by Abstract Expressionism, the Duchampian ethos, neo-Dadaism, and Pop art, Johns is best known for early works that reimagine accessible everyday symbols in order to reassess their value: targets, numerals, and, perhaps most notably, the American flag. These works are now considered among the most influential within the history of postwar art, and have inspired numerous subsequent movements and trends. The seminal *Flag on an Orange Field, II*, 1958, was first displayed at Glenstone in the 2006 *Inaugural Exhibition* and is now on view in Room 2.

–LL

See Also:
Painting (55)
Postwar art (58)
Rauschenberg, Robert (60)

Judd, Donald

b. 1928, d. 1994. American sculptor Donald Judd remains one of the most influential figures in twentieth-century art, and is often associated with the movement known as Minimalism (a categorization about which Judd was rather reluctant). In a seminal 1965 essay titled "Specific Objects," Judd writes that "actual space is intrinsically more powerful and specific than paint on a flat surface," and he developed works intended to exist beyond the strict designations of painting, sculpture, and architecture. *Untitled*, 1963, on view in the Room 2 installation, is an important early piece from a time when Judd was first experimenting with the innovations for which he would become known. Seemingly machine-made, the object is painted but does not hang from a wall, has mass but is not on a pedestal. It sits on the floor almost as a provocation, as though asking: Can this be art?

–AR

See Also:
Minimal art (50)
Sculpture (65)

Integration

Integration indicates the degree to which people, things, ideas, systems, and disciplines are understood as interrelated. At Glenstone our mission is to present art, architecture, and landscape as a seamlessly integrated, holistic experience, aimed at heightening the senses and—ideally—creating meaningful encounters and lasting memories for our visitors. Several outdoor artworks embody this interdisciplinary approach, including Jeff Koons's *Split-Rocker*, 2000 (art, engineering, landscape architecture, horticulture, mosaiculture); Tony Smith's *Smug*, 1973/2005 (art, geometry, paint chemistry, landscape architecture); Andy Goldsworthy's *Clay Houses (Boulder-Room-Holes)*, 2007 (art, architecture, landscape architecture); and Janet Cardiff and George Bures Miller's *FOREST (for a thousand years . . .)*, 2012 (art, music, sound design, landscape architecture).

—EWR and MPR

Kanayama, Akira

b. 1924, d. 2006. Avant-garde Japanese painter Akira Kanayama was a member of the Japanese postwar movement known as Gutai, a community of artists who radically rethought ways of making art. Like Jackson Pollock, whose drip paintings first emerged a decade earlier, and whose works Gutai artists likely saw in reproduction, Kanayama was especially committed to experimenting with process. He is well known for a method that made use of a remote-controlled toy car, to which he would attach a can of paint and then drive across the canvas. *Work*, 1959, on view in the Room 2 installation, was made using this technique. Whereas Pollock's practice emphasized personal expression, Kanayama's tactics remove such implications by creating a painting via purely mechanical means.

–MLe

See Also:
Avant-garde (19)
Gutai (39)
Painting (55)
Process art (59)

Kawara, On

29,771 days. Japanese-born artist On Kawara's work deals with such concepts as consciousness, arbitrariness, and human experience, among others. The Today series, also known as the Date Paintings, are the artist's best-known works; each Date Painting depicts the month, day, and year in which the painting was completed in white paint against a monochromatic background. *Moon Landing*, 1969, on view in the Pavilions, records three key dates of the Apollo 11 space mission: the day the shuttle took off from earth, the day it landed on the moon, and the day Neil Armstrong took his first steps on the moon's surface. For Kawara, making a Date Painting was an act of meditation, a reliable practice in a world filled with uncertainty. Other series, such as I Read, I Met, I Went, I Got Up, and I Am Still Alive, also use objective measures to record various quantities in Kawara's daily life, and are foundational for much Conceptual art that would follow.

–MLe

See Also:
Conceptual art (28–29)

Kelly, Ellsworth

b. 1923, d. 2015. American artist Ellsworth Kelly worked in a range of media, including photography, painting, and sculpture. At forty-five feet high, the commissioned sculpture *Untitled*, 2005, situated directly across from the Gallery Pond, remains one of Kelly's most imposing works. An artist deeply engaged with spatial relations and shadows, Kelly carefully considered the form, material, and placement of this work relative to the surrounding landscape and architecture, and studied the path of the sun throughout the day and its resulting reflection patterns. The sculpture's matte finish is a result of bead-blasting the stainless-steel surface, which appears to change color throughout the day and seasons, consistent with Kelly's long-term interest in nature, light, and color.

–SOw

See Also:
Abstraction (14)
Sculpture (65)
Site-specific (66)
Stainless steel (86)

Kippenberger, Martin

b. 1953, d. 1997. German artist Martin Kippenberger was a prolific and provocative art world presence. Kippenberger was eclectic in both his inspirations—which were literary, popular, and persona—and his output, which encompassed sculpture, painting, drawing, photographs, and prints, among many other forms. Lively and often outrageous, Kippenberger's persona matched the tone of his work, and he welcomed criticism and controversy as further fuel to his artistic identity and production. Kippenberger's sculptural self-portrait *Martin, ab in die Ecke und schäm dich* (Martin, into the Corner, You Should Be Ashamed of Yourself), 1989/1990, was made as a tongue-in-cheek response to his critics, and is on view in the Room 2 installation.

–EG

See Also:
Polke, Sigmar (56)
Postwar art (58)
Sculpture (65)

Klein, Yves

b. 1928, d. 1962. Yves Klein was a French artist associated with the Nouveau Réalisme movement whose works anticipated such major twentieth-century artistic movements as performance art, Conceptualism, Minimalism, and institutional critique. Working across a range of media, Klein used color, particularly a trademark hue of ultramarine known as "International Klein Blue" (IKB), to manifest his notion of "immaterial sensibility," a powerful energy he believed to be present in his work. His striking composition *Untitled Blue Sponge Relief (RE 21)*, 1960, is on view in the Room 2 installation.

–AN

See Also:
Abstraction (14)
Arman (16)
Collage (26)
Nouveau Réalisme (54)
Painting (55)

Kline, Franz

b. 1910, d. 1962. Though American painter Franz Kline trained as an illustrator and produced representational works early on in his career, he is best known for his large black-and-white abstract "action" paintings. Like his fellow Abstract Expressionists, Kline employed bold, energetic brushstrokes and often used ordinary house paint, though *Untitled*, 1957, on view in the Room 2 installation, employs oil on canvas. *Untitled* is deceiving in its appearance of spontaneity; starting with a primed canvas and alternating between black and white, Kline mixed the paint directly on the surface in a purposefully uneven application. The result is a dynamic blend of scumbling and impasto, gloss passages and matte ones. The thick, textured black brushstrokes almost vibrate with energy; in contrast, the white paint appears calmly placed around and within the fields of black.

–FG

See Also:
Abstract Expressionism (14–15)
Painting (55)

Koons, Jeff

b. 1955. Jeff Koons is one of America's most recognizable, prolific, and polarizing artists. Known for paintings and sculptures that depict pop-cultural touchstones, Koons draws on a deep understanding of art historical trends and precedents. His oeuvre has been interpreted variously as trailblazing or as kitsch, and Koons is deeply engaged in issues surrounding commodification and consumerism. Koon's outdoor sculpture *Split-Rocker*, 2000, visible at the Pavilions entrance, consists of thousands of living plants and flowers, replanted at Glenstone once every year. A topiary with conceptual roots in neo-Impressionist pointillism, *Split-Rocker* exemplifies Koons's affinity for color, recognizable form, and the big and bright.

—NSC

See Also:
Mosaiculture (104)
New Guinea impatiens
    (*Impatiens hawkeri*) (102)
Sculpture (65)
Stainless steel (86)

Kruger, Barbara

b. 1945. American artist Barbara Kruger works, in her own words, "with pictures and words." Kruger's methodology merges techniques from commercial and fine art, combining a signature bold typeface—reminiscent of advertising headlines—with popular images to examine power and gender stereotypes. Kruger has an abiding interest in critiquing cultural and political conventions, and frequently creates a sense of tension between the literal and figurative by superimposing text onto seemingly unrelated appropriated imagery. *Untitled (We won't play nature to your culture)*, 1983, on view in the Room 2 installation, exemplifies this direct, impactful style.

—CD

See Also:
Appropriation art (16–17)
Conceptual art (28–29)
Photography (55)
Pop art (56)

Kusama, Yayoi

b. 1929. Artist Yayoi Kusama moved from Japan to New York in the late 1950s, quickly becoming one of the most daring participants in the local avant-garde art scene. Her Accumulations, a series of soft sculptures begun in the early 1960s, covered various furniture items with stuffed phallic forms, and were seen by the artist as a way to concretize and subjugate her anxieties about sex. Artmaking has been a lifelong mode of inquiry and catharsis for Kusama, who notes that hallucinations have inspired many of her now-iconic motifs—from polka dots to pumpkins to her immersive infinity-mirror installations. The white-painted *Accumulation on Cabinet No. 1*, 1963, on view in the Room 2 installation, is covered in phallic protrusions stuck on and around the shelves of a cabinet stacked high with cups and glasses and "fenced in" by chicken wire.

—KV

See Also:
Assemblage (18)
Avant-garde (19)

Kusama, Yayoi

LeWitt, Sol

b. 1928, d. 2007. American artist Sol LeWitt's interest in analyzing pure geometric forms often aligns him with the Minimalist movement, while his pioneering theories of art also place him at the forefront of the movement that became known as Conceptualism. Working with simple shapes like squares, circles, and triangles, LeWitt examined the very nature of art, shifting the emphasis from execution to idea: his famous dictum that "the idea becomes the machine that makes the art" quickly became artistic gospel (both revered and renounced) after he wrote the statement in his essay "Paragraphs on Conceptual Art," published in Artforum in 1967. LeWitt first gained attention in the 1960s for sculptures built according to simple mathematical progressions, theoretical frameworks that could be understood and executed by anyone. These works were made with common materials and a limited color palette of red, blue, yellow, and black, such as *Run IV*, 1962, on view in the Room 2 installation.

As he continued to work, LeWitt further "dematerialized" his sculptures, creating instructions for his drawings to be executed by others directly on gallery walls.

–EM

See Also:
Conceptual art (28–29)
Hesse, Eva (40–41)
Minimal art (50)

Marden, Brice

b. 1938. Long captivated by color and its ability to forge emotional connections, American painter Brice Marden rose to prominence following a series of early monochromatic panel paintings rendered in oil and beeswax. Repeated trips to Greece led to a lifelong interest in capturing light, and a curiosity about Chinese calligraphy and philosophy prompted his inquiry into the practice of energetic mark-making. Marden has been described as a "romantic Minimalist," and is expressive in his paint application, often leaving traces of his hand embedded in the work. The multipanel *Moss Sutra with the Seasons*, 2010–2015, commissioned by Glenstone and on view in the Pavilions, is the result of five years of work, and fuses essential elements of Marden's practice: color, light, and energy.

–AL

See Also:
Abstraction (14)
Commission (28)
Drawing (32–33)
Painting (55)
Pavilions, the (83)

Design

Every detail of Glenstone embodies our design ethos, which is in large part inspired by architect Ludwig Mies van der Rohe's dictum "less is more." Visitors to Glenstone may notice that each building is constructed out of only a few materials: teak, granite, and zinc for the Gallery, and maple, concrete, and stainless steel for the Pavilions. We have paid special attention to the integrity of the materials, so that surfaces read as authentic yet refined. The same principles guide the design of the amenities and touch points, including the furniture, fixtures, uniforms, and signage, all of which are intended to recede into the background after performing their respective functions, quietly supporting your experience with art, architecture, and landscape. Throughout the property, materials were selected in a restrained color palette of silver, black, white, and buff, in addition to Glenstone Gray, a shade mixed especially for us by Pantone, the international color-systems manufacturer.

–EWR and MPR

Martin, Agnes

b. 1912, d. 2004. Born in Canada, Agnes Martin was an American painter whose work is radically spare, as demonstrated by the nearly imperceptible hand-drawn graphite grid of *Pilgrimage*, 1966, currently on view in the Room 2 installation. While often described as a Minimalist, Martin in fact felt a kinship with Abstract Expressionism, and attempted to transcend materiality and engage broader universal themes in her work. In the late 1960s, she left New York and traveled before ultimately landing in remote New Mexico. There she ceased painting for a time, only to "reemerge" in 1974 with a new body of work that included subtle strips of pale colors. She lived alone for the rest of her life in the Southwestern desert, quietly demonstrating a thoughtful humility and steadfast devotion to her work.

—MLe

See Also:
Abstraction (14)
Minimal art (50)
Painting (55)
Postwar art (58)

Merz, Marisa

b. 1926. Italian artist Marisa Merz's work spans a broad range of media, including drawing, painting, and sculpture. Merz also worked with a wide and idiosyncratic array of materials, such as woven copper wire, monofilament, and aluminum sheeting, which she used in abundance to create sculptures, often in her kitchen at home in Turin. Versatile and unbound by convention, Merz created both small- and large-scale works, from delicate sculpted clay heads to massive painted installations that encompass entire walls. Married to fellow artist Mario Merz, she was the only female member of the Arte Povera movement in postwar Italy. Her sensibility, however, remains entirely singular, as is evident in the work *Untitled*, 1977, currently on view in the Room 2 installation.

—SOw

See Also:
Arte Povera (18)
Installation (42)
Painting (55)
Sculpture (65)

Minimal Art

Minimalism first emerged as a movement advanced by a group of American artists in the 1950s, intent on pushing past the expressionism of their celebrated (Abstract Expressionist) predecessors. Even if many resisted the label, the best-known artists associated with Minimalism—such as Carl Andre, Jo Baer, Dan Flavin, Donald Judd, and Frank Stella—rebelled against Abstract Expressionism's lush, colorful surfaces by employing simple geometric forms, repetition, and industrial materials. Minimalist artworks often demonstrate a straightforward, clean aesthetic; "what you see is what you see," Stella famously declared in relation to his series of Black Paintings, now recognized as some of the movement's first major artistic statements. One of these paintings, *Bethlehem's Hospital*, 1959, is on view in the Room 2 installation, as are other works by the artists mentioned above.

—AN

See Also:
Baer, Jo (19)

Martin, Agnes

Modern Art

A term generally invoked in conjunction with certain art movements developed from the late nineteenth century onwards, including Impressionism, Cubism, Surrealism, Bauhaus, Futurism, Abstract Expressionism, and Pop art. Modern art emphasizes innovation and experimentation in forms, materials, and techniques, with a general aim to create works that reflect the conditions of modern society. Glenstone's collection encompasses many artists who worked in conversation with modernist ideals or tendencies.

–NR

See Also:
Beuys, Joseph (20–21)
Bourgeois, Louise (22–23)
Camargo, Sergio (24)
Giacometti, Alberto (36)
Rothko, Mark (64)

Motonaga, Sadamasa

b. 1922, d. 2011. Japanese artist Sadamasa Motonaga developed a passion for manga—Japanese comics—as a child, a passion that would remain throughout his life and influence his work along the way. In the early 1950s, Motonaga exhibited an artwork at the 6th Ashiya City Art Exhibition, at which he came across abstract art for the first time. This proved to be a particularly significant moment, prompting his own shift toward the abstractions for which he would eventually become known. After joining the Gutai group in 1955, Motonaga continued to experiment, using amorphous materials such as water and smoke. *Sakuhin*, 1962, on view in the Room 2 installation, exemplifies a technique the artist developed in which various colors of paint are poured onto the canvas in layers.

–KN

See Also:
Gutai (39)
Kanayama, Akira (44)
Painting (55)
Process art (59)
Shimamoto, Shozo (66–67)

Nauman, Bruce

b. 1941. The works of American artist Bruce Nauman span a diverse range of media, from photography and drawing to video and neon. *American Violence*, 1981–1982, on view in the Room 2 installation, consists of eight words or phrases rendered in neon in the shape of a swastika. All components of the light fixtures are intentionally visible to the viewer: the power station with its Plexiglas cover, the transformer, and four short power cables. The voltage applied to the neon glass tubes causes different mixtures of gas to emit light in various colors; as *American Violence* flashes on and off we see phrases both ominous and absurd, as though illuminated on the Vegas strip. The works remains unsettlingly relevant today, almost forty years after it was made.

–SO

See Also:
Conservation (30–31)
Flavin, Dan (34)
Light (82–83)
Post-Minimal art (58)

Modern art

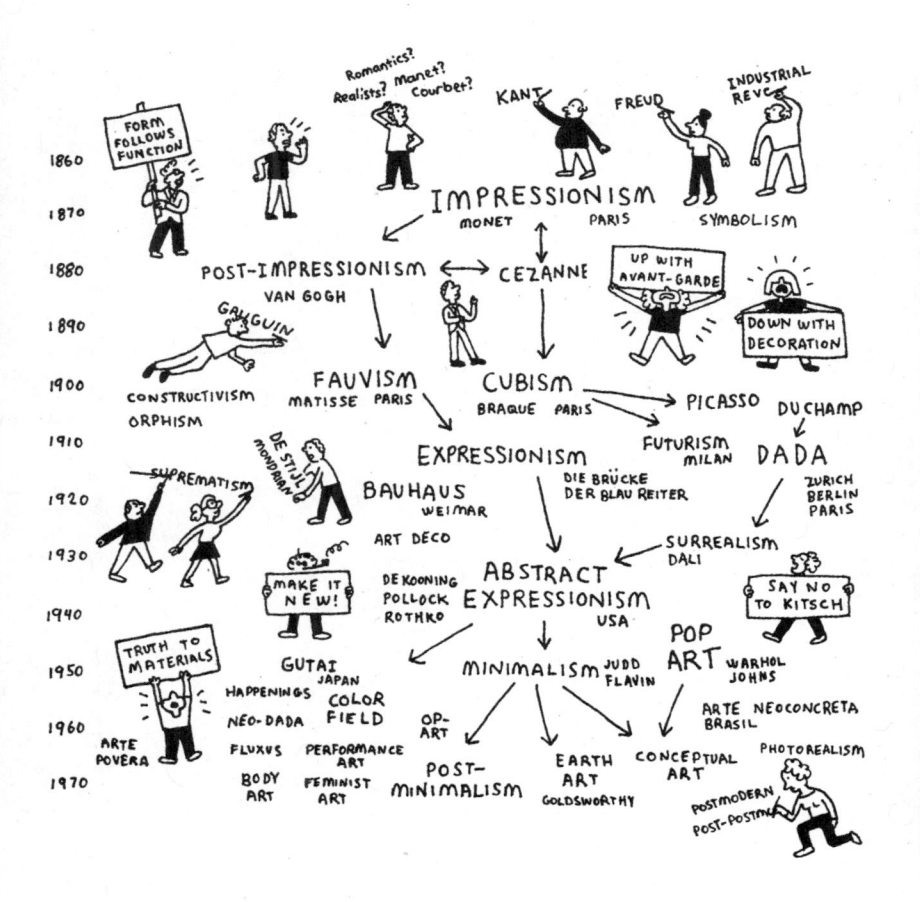

Nouveau Réalisme

In 1960 Pierre Restany, a French art critic, organized an exhibition at the Galleria Apollinaire in Milan, bringing together the work of such artists as Arman, Christo, Yves Klein, and Jean Tinguely under the moniker *Nouveau Réalisme*, or "new realism." The Nouveau Réalistes took a special interest in discarded materials and found inspiration in the banal grittiness of industrialized urban life. Rope, fabric, dinner plates, posters, car parts, cans, and many other quotidian found objects were given new life in the form of collage, assemblage, and painting. Restany championed these works, which brought the material of everyday life and art closer together, as a "new way of perceiving the real."

–EM

See Also:
Arman (16)
Assemblage (18)
Avant-garde (19)
Klein, Yves (45)
Readymade (60–61)
Tinguely, Jean (70)

Oiticica, Hélio

b. 1937, d. 1980. Brazilian artist Hélio Oiticica worked across various media, including painting, sculpture, and documentary film. A member of the movement known as Arte Neoconcreta, Oiticica often used primary colors and elementary shapes to create nuanced artworks and architectural sculptures. He also created large-scale environments for viewers to enter into and interact with, effectively allowing them to become a part of the work. *Relevo espacial (amarelo)* (Spatial relief [yellow]), 1960, on view in the Room 2 installation, is painted a vivid yellow and installed as a floating shape off the wall. Like Oiticica's larger environments, this piece draws the audience close to and around it, creating a dialogue where person, object, and environment form a special, even symbiotic, relationship.

–SHS

See Also:
Arte Neoconcreta (16)
Camargo, Sergio (24)
Clark, Lygia (26)
Pape, Lygia (55)
Sculpture (65)

Oldenburg, Claes

b. 1929. While Swedish-American artist Claes Oldenburg is especially well known for producing monumental sculptures of commonplace items, in 1961 Oldenburg staged a now-famous experimental installation titled *The Store*, where he "stocked" a commercial storefront with gloopy plaster re-creations of modestly sized consumer products. Over the course of a few months, Oldenburg sold these sculptures at affordable prices, replacing items as they were purchased. Turning the idea of an "art market" on its head, *The Store* is now considered landmark moment in the history of Pop art; *Cash Register*, 1961, on view the Room 2 installation, was created as a part of this early project.

–MLe

See Also:
Sculpture (65)
Warhol, Andy (72)

Painting

Paintings are, broadly speaking, produced by applying pigment suspended in a binder to a surface using any of a variety of mark-making tools—brushes, fingers, squeegees, sponges, and so forth. Glenstone's collection includes works made with oil paint on canvas—a classic technique—but also works composed with mud on canvas, acrylic on drywall, beeswax on panel, and many other combinations. In Yves Klein's *Untitled Blue Sponge Relief (RE 21)*, 1960, on view in the Room 2 installation, for example, natural sponges and pebbles are placed on the board and painted over with the artist's iconic blue pigment.

—SOw

See Also:
Abstract Expressionism (14–15)
Gutai (39)
Klein, Yves (45)

Pape, Lygia

b. 1927, d. 2004. Brazilian artist Lygia Pape is known for highly politicized work across a range of media, including sculpture, engraving, performance, and film. In direct reaction to the Brazilian Concrete art movement of the 1950s, which decreed that art objects had no meaning beyond their physicality, Pape joined several well-known contemporaries to form the Arte Neoconcreta movement, which emphasized the poetic, the personal, and the engagement of the viewer as integral components of artmaking. *Livro do Tempo I* (The Book of Time I), 1961, on view in Room 9 in the Pavilions, is composed of 365 unique wooden objects, or "pages," representing each day of the year. Using primary colors and geometric sequences, Pape invites the viewer to create their own reading of the passage of time.

—NSC

See Also:
Abstraction (14)
Arte Neoconcreta (16)
Clark, Lygia (26)
Oiticica, Hélio (54)
Schendel, Mira (65)

Photography

Photography, a method of recording an image using light, derives its name from the Greek words for light (*phos*) and to draw (*graphein*). The relatively short exposure times of the daguerreotype, an early photographic process developed by Louis-Jacques-Mandé Daguerre in the 1830s, and, later, the convenience of roll film, widely distributed by Eastman Kodak Company, helped popularize the medium. Photography was enthusiastically used to capture landscapes, document new cultures, and assist in scientific endeavors; however, it wasn't considered a proper art form (even though artists were early adopters of the medium) until the twentieth century, when photography began to garner some of the respect traditionally bestowed on painting and sculpture. Just as the photographic process continued to evolve over time—most notably with the advent of digital technology—so has the use of photography as an artistic medium, as seen in the photographic silkscreen *Untitled (We won't play nature to your culture)*, 1983, by Barbara Kruger, on view in the Room 2 installation.

—FG

Polke, Sigmar

b. 1941, d. 2010. Born in East Germany, multifaceted painter Sigmar Polke came to prominence along with fellow German artists Gerhard Richter and Konrad Lueg in the early 1960s, as part of a movement they christened "Capitalist Realism." The movement was in many ways a send-up of American Pop art; Polke's early works engage the commodification of objects and advertising culture without Pop's flashy sheen. His paintings of sausages and chocolate (highly prized items in postwar Germany) are darkly humorous, flat, and expressionless, as though one is seeing enlarged and slightly skewed newspaper ads rendered by hand. Two of his most renowned paintings from this era, *Schokoladenbild* (Chocolate Painting), 1964, and *Der Wurstesser* (The Sausage Eater), 1963, are on view in the Room 2 installation.

—CD

See Also:
Painting (55)
Pop art (56)
Postwar art (58)

Pollock, Jackson

b. 1912, d. 1956. Jackson Pollock was an American painter and arguably *the* key figure in the Abstract Expressionist movement. Throughout his career the artist experimented with a range of approaches to drawing and painting; however, Pollock is best known for developing the technique of "drip painting," where he would place a canvas directly on the floor and control the flow of paint on it from above. The process balanced a singular approach to materials, improvisation, and chance to create some of the most iconic works of the last century. *Number 1*, 1952, is on view in the Room 2 installation.

—AN

See Also:
Abstract Expressionism (14–15)
Abstraction (14)
Avant-garde (19)
Painting (55)
Process art (59)

Pop Art

An influential art movement that emerged in Britain and the United States in the 1950s, Pop art blossomed more fully in the 1960s as a direct response to these countries' unprecedented economic and political successes in the years following World War II. Pop art attempted to critically engage with—and even subvert—a supposed trend of societal and economic conformity, melding "high art" with the traditionally low, aestheticizing familiar objects with references to advertising and commercial culture. Often making use of kitsch, primary colors, and multiples—as seen in the work of several of the movement's most iconic figures, such as Andy Warhol and Roy Lichtenstein—Pop art deconstructed the boundaries between art and media, and charted a new direction for art as the heyday of Abstract Expressionism was beginning to fade.

—CD

See Also:
Oldenburg, Claes (54)
Postmodern art (58)
Printmaking (59)
Warhol, Andy (72)

Pollock, Jackson

Post-Minimal Art

A term coined by Robert Pincus-Witten to encapsulate a broad range of related artistic styles that took root in the United States in the late 1960s, post-Minimalism is frequently thought of as a reaction to Minimal art's adherence to rigid geometric constraints, advocating instead for more open and expressive forms. Post-Minimalist artists frequently used unconventional materials such as latex, rubber, aluminum, and neon lights, as seen in works by Lynda Benglis, Eva Hesse, Bruce Nauman, and Richard Serra, respectively, all on view in the Room 2 installation. Post-Minimalists also employed a wide array of modes of expression, including performance and body art, Land art, and process art.

—SE

See Also:
Benglis, Lynda (20)
Hesse, Eva (40–41)
Minimal art (50)
Nauman, Bruce (52)
Serra, Richard (65)

Postmodern Art

A highly debated term, art deemed postmodern often corresponds to a particular time frame rather than a specific style. The period generally associated with postmodern art follows the late-1960s rise of a group of French philosophers (including Jean Baudrillard and Jean-François Lyotard, who questioned the foundations of dominant Western hierarchical thought), reaching its apex in the 1970s and 1980s, when art employing strategies of appropriation, quotation, and pastiche flourished. Although postmodern art has no singular defining visual style, it is typically made in deliberate reaction to the general ideals of modernism, including, for example, a rejection of the primacy of originality and of the artist's individuality.

—ET

See Also:
Arte Povera (18)
Conceptual art (28–29)
Pop art (56)

Postwar Art

In art history, the term *postwar* generally refers to the period following World War II and spans a broad range of movements, including Abstract Expressionism, Minimalism, post-Minimalism, Pop art, Conceptual art, Arte Povera, and Fluxus. The focus of Glenstone's collection is on postwar artists, and a wide range of pioneering works from the period are currently on view. From Jackson Pollock's explosion of gestural paint on canvas to Eva Hesse's sculptural innovations using fiberglass and latex, artwork produced during this time creates a complicated and sometimes contradictory portrait of art—and of the rich, dynamic, and often difficult history that binds it.

—MLe

See Also:
Abstract Expressionism (14–15)
Arte Neoconcreta (16)
Arte Povera (18)
Gutai (39)
Minimal art (50)
Pop art (56)

Printmaking

Printmaking is a broad term referencing art made through a multistep reproductive process in which an intermediary plane is used to transfer an image to the final surface. Some methods, such as engraving, allow multiple prints to be made using a single plate; other methods, such as monotype, result in unique works. They all share the use of a base (typically a plate, surface, or object) and pigment, often employ pressure, and generally fall within three categories: relief, in which the image is raised above the printing surface; intaglio, in which the image is etched into the plate's surface; and planographic, in which the image remains flat on the printing surface. From Paleolithic handprints and stencil art to contemporary hand-finished digital prints, the history of printmaking spans millennia and remains a vital and dynamic part of twenty-first-century art practice. The silk-screening technique can be seen in Andy Warhol's *Large Flowers*, 1964, on view in the Room 2 installation.

–CG

See Also:
Bourgeois, Louise (22–23)
Kruger, Barbara (46)
Warhol, Andy (72)

Process Art

In the 1960s and 1970s, artists began experimenting with new processes for creating art, including the use of materials that were nontraditional, malleable, and fluid. Lynda Benglis's polyurethane pieces, Eva Hesse's latex sculptures, Robert Morris's felt works, and Richard Serra's Belts reveal the eccentric forms that resulted from such experiments, in which the use of gravity often played a role in shaping and manipulating the final artwork. The goal of these artists was not to make perfect objects, but to engage in a process of making that would itself be embedded in the work's finished aesthetic. Many pieces on view at Glenstone can be classified as process art—which as a category often indicates a shared disposition rather than inclusion in an official movement—including Benglis's cast-aluminum sculpture *WING*, 1970, on view in the Room 2 installation.

–CD

See Also:
Benglis, Lynda (20)
Hesse, Eva (40–41)
Serra, Richard (65)

Public Art

In its most general sense, public art refers to any artwork that has been planned and executed with the intention of being embedded within the public sphere. In practice, public art is often site-specific, outdoors, and accessible. Historically, much public art has been militaristic in nature, with monuments, memorials, and statues erected to celebrate victories and political and civic leaders. As political, social, and cultural climates grow increasingly complex, public art has come to rely more heavily on visual artists who register current events or use their work to rally for a specific cause. David Hammons's *How Ya Like Me Now?*, 1988, is an example in Glenstone's collection of a work created for the public sphere—and originally shown in downtown Washington, DC.

–NSC

See Also:
Commission (28)
Hammons, David (39)
Sculpture (65)
Site-specific (66)

Puryear, Martin

b. 1941. American artist Martin Puryear was born in Washington, DC, and works primarily with materials such as wood, stone, and metal. Puryear studied traditional crafts in Sierra Leone while in the Peace Corps, printmaking at the Royal Swedish Academy of Arts in Stockholm, and sculpture at Yale University. Puryear is perhaps best known for his works in wood, which range from organic forms inspired by nature to abstracted representational objects. *Big Phrygian*, 2010–2014, and *The Load*, 2012, on view in the Passage in the Pavilions, are examples of the latter. Made of several different types of wood—pine, red cedar, ash, and maple—as well as steel and glass, the work incorporates a found carriage with a sculpture of a giant eye inside. Puryear also collaborated with furniture fabricator Michael Hurwitz on the centerpiece bench in the viewing gallery, made of hickory with a maple veneer.

–KB

See Also:
Commission (28)
Sculpture (65)
Wood (89–91)

Rauschenberg, Robert

b. 1925, d. 2008. Coca-Cola bottles, a worn pair of boots, a clock, and a small ceramic dog, all placed on and around a gold Japanese folding screen, are just some of the elements in American artist Robert Rauschenberg's *Gold Standard*, 1964, on view in the Room 2 installation. Originally created during a four-hour artist talk–turned–improvised performance in Tokyo on November 28, 1964, *Gold Standard* is the final work produced as part of Rauschenberg's revolutionary Combine series (1954–1964). The Combines are seen as a significant moment in postwar American art, as Rauschenberg extended the painterly gestures of Abstract Expressionism into three-dimensional painting-sculpture hybrids, incorporating found materials and setting the stage for Pop art.

–CD

See Also:
Appropriation art (16–17)
Assemblage (18)
Pop art (56)

Puryear, Martin

Ray, Charles

b. 1953. The work of American artist Charles Ray is difficult to categorize; his diverse practice spans different media, subject matter, styles, and concepts. Ray began his artistic career under the tutelage of the sculptor Roland Brener at the University of Iowa. During this time, he was exposed to the works of English sculptor Anthony Caro and to concepts such as tension, seriality, and balance. This formalist language is evident in Ray's exploration of perspective, his handling of materials, and his conceptualization of form within a surrounding space. *Baled Truck*, 2014, one of several works by the artist on view in the Pavilions, is a sculpture of a large truck compressed into a tight block: though it appears to have been compacted by a junkyard-style car crusher, in fact the thirteen-ton sculpture was machined from solid stainless steel.

–JSh

See Also:
Pavilions, the (83)
Sculpture (65)
Stainless steel (86)

Readymade

The term *readymade*, coined by French artist Marcel Duchamp in the early 1900s, denotes artworks that are minimally altered, mass-produced found objects; removed from their original contexts, these objects gain new meaning when designated as artworks. Duchamp's readymades challenged the conventional ideas that art should be beautiful and made by the artist's hand, instead placing emphasis on the idea behind the artwork and ultimately paving the way for the emergence of Conceptual art. Two of Duchamp's earliest and most infamous readymades are on view in the Room 2 installation—*Roue de Bicyclette*, 1913/1964, and *Fountain*, 1917/1964.

Over time, the term has broadened to include the more general use of found or manufactured objects as art material, such as the glasses, bottles, and kitchen cabinet in Yayoi Kusama's *Accumulation on Cabinet No. 1*, 1963.

–AL

See Also:
Arman (16)
Avant-garde (19)
Conceptual art (28–29)
Duchamp, Marcel (32)

Readymade

Rist, Pipilotti

b. 1962. Pipilotti Rist is a Swiss visual artist and filmmaker known for pioneering short-length, engrossing video artworks and multimedia installations. For many of her most recognizable films she employed herself as director, producer, star, and composer, an ongoing practice that reflects her varied interests in human emotion, female sexuality, psychology, music, and her own body. By keeping her videos short, Rist is mimicking the bite-size nature of commercial culture and the manic attention span of a generation raised on MTV. Over and over, she forces viewers to reconcile the juxtaposition between what they see and how they feel. Composed with the intent of relaxing the viewer with playful music while showcasing a joyful act of repeated vandalism, the surreal and analog *Ever Is Over All*, 1997, is presented in Room 6 of the Pavilions. Widely considered an iconic feminist statement, the work served as inspiration for Beyoncé's 2016 music video *Hold Up*. For art critic Peter Schjeldahl, "anarchy has never been so honey-sweet."

–NSC

Roth, Dieter

b. 1930, d. 1998. Swiss artist Dieter Roth is one of the most prolific users of food as an artistic medium. Weighing in at 816 pounds, *Herd* (Stove), 1969, on view in the Room 2 installation, consists of melted chocolate oozing out of a previously used wood-fired kitchen stove. The stove rests on a wooden stand with black handles, which Roth considered part of the work. The melted chocolate became hard and brittle over time, and small holes—where insects eventually burrowed through—remain visible on its surface. The artist embraced this decay, accepting these changes as part of the work. While a preoccupation with entropy is one of the cornerstones of Roth's work, for a conservator it makes things even more intriguing: if an infestation were to occur, any resulting markings from either the infestation or its eradication would, according to the artist, become part of the official work.

–SO

See Also:
Post-Minimal art (58)
Process art (59)

Rothko, Mark

b. 1903, d. 1970. Born in Latvia as Markus Yakovlevich Rothkowitz, American painter Mark Rothko is widely recognized for developing now-iconic large-scale Color Field paintings, in which layered rectangles seem to both recede into and emerge out of vast fields of contrasting colors. His unique paint application involved thinly layered hues and broad brushstrokes, and his large canvases can feel expansive and evocative, luminous and sensual. Rothko strove to engage certain universal tensions in his work, such as tragedy, irony, and wit, and he wished for his paintings to provide an immersive, intimate experience for the viewer. The large and enveloping *No. 9 (White and Black on Wine)*, 1958, is on view in the Room 2 installation.

–PI

See Also:
Abstract Expressionism (14–15)
Modern art (52–53)
Painting (55)

Schendel, Mira

b. 1919, d. 1988. Artist Mira Schendel spent her early years in Europe before moving to Brazil in the late 1940s, and displacement—both geographical and metaphorical—is a recurring motif throughout her work. Often contextualized within the geometric abstraction espoused by Brazilian modernism, her works are abstract, minimal, formalist, and entirely handmade. Famous for her Monotypes (drawings created by scoring translucent Japanese rice paper with her fingernails) and her series Graphic Objects (large swaths of rice paper with nonsensical lettering and poetry written across each side, hung between transparent acrylic sheets), Schendel's work is deeply rooted in her personal sense of self. Three of her Graphic Objects, dating from 1960 to 1972, are on view in the Room 2 installation.

–NSC

See Also:
Abstraction (14)
Clark, Lygia (26)
Drawing (32–33)
Oiticica, Hélio (54)
Postwar art (58)

Sculpture

Whether carved, cast, molded, assembled, or constructed, sculpture allows the viewer to go beyond single-point perspective and experience a work three-dimensionally through shifting points of view. At Glenstone sculptures are presented without stanchions or barriers, granting visitors the freedom of movement to fully absorb a work's presence in its given space or location. Walk around and observe the many sides from different standpoints. Encompass the work. Let it encompass you.

–SW

See Also:
Goldsworthy, Andy (36–37)
Horn, Roni (40)
Koons, Jeff (46)
Serra, Richard (65)
Sight line (105)
Smith, Tony (68)

Serra, Richard

b. 1938. American sculptor Richard Serra's interest in steel grew from his early visits to scrap metal yards and boatyards. The use of this industrial material as a malleable medium, which can be manipulated to produce seemingly fluid forms, became Serra's hallmark, exemplified by the weathering-steel outdoor sculptures *Sylvester*, 2001, at the Gallery's entrance, and *Contour 290*, 2004, which was commissioned by Glenstone. Throughout his prolific career, Serra has also worked in a multitude of unconventional materials such as vulcanized rubber, neon tubing, and lead, as seen in *White Neon Belt Piece* and *To Lift*, both 1967, and *Corner Prop*, 1969, on view in the Room 2 installation.

–AL

See Also:
Meadow (103)
Sculpture (65)
Sight line (105)
Site-specific (66)

Shimamoto, Shozo

b. 1928, d. 2013. Shozo Shimamoto was a Japanese artist and cofounder of the avant-garde Gutai group, as well as a key figure in Japanese correspondence art. Like many of his Gutai peers, Shimamoto was focused on the unique physicality of materials and on processes that pushed beyond traditional techniques or forms. His works often bear the imprint of the active—and almost violent—practices of their making, such as *Untitled (White)*, 1955, on view in the Room 2 installation. Part of a series of works involving punctures to the support, this piece was built up using layers of newspaper that Shimamoto painted, a process that eventually tore holes through the papers' hardened surface. The artist has written that "even if my method seems shocking . . . because I am an artist my purpose is to make the work beautiful, to show the beauty of everything."

–AR

See Also:
Avant-garde (19)
Gutai (39)
Painting (55)
Postwar art (58)

Shiraga, Kazuo

b. 1924, d. 2008. Having originally trained in the traditional Japanese painting practice of *nihonga*, artist Kazuo Shiraga eventually joined the radical Gutai group in postwar Japan. For Shiraga, the body itself was a primary vehicle for artistic expression, and he developed an idiosyncratic, vigorous approach to making that synthesized both painting and performance. Placing a canvas on the floor, Shiraga would suspend himself from the ceiling by rope, using only his feet to manipulate large swaths of paint on its surface. The direct connection between body and material was key, and the resulting surfaces remain some of the most tempestuous and dynamic of late twentieth-century abstraction. An early painting made using this method, *Untitled*, 1958, is on view in the Room 2 installation.

–AR

See Also:
Abstraction (14)
Avant-garde (19)
Gutai (39)
Painting (55)
Postwar art (58)

Site-Specific

A term prevalent in artistic discourse since the 1970s, *site-specific* refers to artwork conceptualized and created in direct relationship to its location (whether geographic, institutional, environmental, or social). The phrase gained notice in the controversy surrounding Richard Serra's *Tilted Arc*, 1981, a sculpture originally installed at Federal Plaza at Foley Square in downtown New York. Protestors petitioned for the artwork's removal, arguing that the work disrupted public use of the space. Serra maintained that *Tilted Arc* "is a site-specific work and as such it is not to be relocated. To remove the work is to destroy the work." At Glenstone, the commissioned outdoor sculpture *Contour 290*, 2004, is site-specific.

–AR

See Also:
Commission (28)
Goldsworthy, Andy (36–37)
Kelly, Ellsworth (44)
Sculpture (65)
Serra, Richard (65)

Shiraga, Kazuo

Smith, Tony

b. 1912, d. 1980. Tony Smith was an iconic American artist best known for large-scale Minimalist sculptures made of industrial materials. Smith's *Smug*, 1973/2005, exemplifies the style of geometric abstraction most characteristic of his work, and is prominently installed on the grounds at Glenstone. The artist originally built a plywood mockup of this piece in his New Jersey backyard; while the intended painted aluminum version was never completed during his lifetime, Glenstone manifested this final version working in close collaboration with the artist's family.

–AH

See Also:
Abstraction (14)
Framed views (78–79)
Minimal art (50)
Sculpture (65)

Sound Art

Sound art provides an experience that relies primarily on the audience's sense of hearing. The sound can encompass anything from recognizable musical notes, spoken words, and background noise to silence, ambient atmospheric rumblings, and barely perceptible vibrations. Artists variously use the medium of sound to produce an emotional response, visceral reaction, memory, or confusion in the audience. Often the auditory experience, though primary, is not the only focus of sound art: installations can involve visual, spatial, or other physical and sensory considerations. One example of sound art in Glenstone's collection is Janet Cardiff and George Bures Miller's *FOREST (for a thousand years . . .)*, 2012.

–MC

See Also:
Cardiff, Janet and George Bures Miller (26–27)
Installation (42)
Time-based media (69)

Stella, Frank

b. 1936. American artist Frank Stella first gained recognition for a series of symmetrical, monochromatic canvases he made between 1959 and 1960, now collectively known as the Black Paintings. These paintings were executed in regular two-and-a-half-inch strokes in black enamel paint, with a thin line of canvas left bare between each strip; Stella's innovation with this approach was in creating a "non-relational" painting—in other words, a painting where no one section commanded more attention than any other. The Black Paintings are now seen by many as the decisive hinge between modernism and the Minimalist movement that emerged during the later half of the twentieth century; one of these early paintings, *Bethlehem's Hospital*, 1959, is on view in the Room 2 installation. The title is a reference to the infamous psychiatric hospital in London more commonly known as Bedlam.

–JSh

See Also:
Abstraction (14)
Minimal art (50)
Painting (55)

Still, Clyfford

b. 1904, d. 1980. A pioneer of postwar American painting, Clyfford Still was one of the first Abstract Expressionists to shift away from the representational and embrace nonfigurative abstraction. Some have seen natural phenomena—caves or flames—in Still's colorful, riotous canvases, and the artist relied heavily on vertical forms to explore a tension between the human spirit and forces of nature (Still spoke of the "vertical necessity of life"). Though he was an active participant in New York's vibrant 1950s art scene, Still eventually grew disillusioned with the art world and left New York to settle on a farm in Carroll County, Maryland, where he remained—and painted—for the rest of his life. His *1949-A, No. 2*, 1949, is on view in the Room 2 installation.

–SW

See Also:
Abstract Expressionism (14–15)
Painting (55)

Tanaka, Atsuko

b. 1932, d. 2005. Atsuko Tanaka was a pioneering artist whose work gained prominence as part of a flourishing Japanese avant-garde following World War II. Tanaka's most iconic work involves performance; her *Electric Dress*, 1956, created while she was a member of the groundbreaking Gutai group, was a wearable shift made from flashing electric lights in red, yellow, blue, and green, wired together and plugged into the wall. From the 1960s onward Tanaka produced mainly abstract paintings, whose color and composition often recall the *Electric Dress*'s tangled and vibrant web. *WORK*, 1963, on view in the Room 2 installation, demonstrates the playfulness and rigor of Tanaka's practice—at once organic and ordered, a mix of chaos and harmony.

–AR

See Also:
Avant-garde (19)
Gutai (39)
Painting (55)
Postwar art (58)

Time-based Media

Time-based media is a broad, all-inclusive term used to describe the field of art production in which duration is a fundamental characteristic. Digitally produced art employing video, sound, and software is frequently included in the category of time-based media; kinetic sculpture and performance art are classified as time-based media as well, because temporal change is integral to such works. An example of time-based media at Glenstone is the outdoor sound installation *FOREST (for a thousand years . . .)*, 2012, by Janet Cardiff and George Bures Miller, which plays on a continuous twenty-eight-minute loop along the woodland trail. Conservation of time-based media is a developing practice that requires a nimble response to the impending obsolescence of technologies and methods, such as digitizing videos recorded on VHS tapes or documenting code written for a software-based work.

–SOw

See Also:
Contemporary art (30)
Conservation (30–31)
Rist, Pipilotti (64)

Tinguely, Jean

b. 1925, d. 1991. Swiss artist Jean Tinguely began making assemblage sculptures from found objects in the mid-1940s. Inspired by the rapid industrialization around him, the artist soon introduced mechanical movement to his sculptures—often creating works that could be animated by movement and subsequently self-destruct, like Glenstone's *Grande Méta-Mecanique No. 1*, 1955. The artist described these works as "metamatic," laying the groundwork for a movement which subsequently became known as kinetic art.

–AN

See Also:
Assemblage (18)
Nouveau Réalisme (54)
Sculpture (65)

Trockel, Rosemarie

b. 1952. German artist Rosemarie Trockel's diverse practice draws from a variety of sources, including text, technology, natural history, politics, and popular culture. While her oeuvre includes film, video, ceramics, clothing, drawing, collage, and sculpture, she is best known for her knitted paintings, which engage both the history of the Cold War and deep-seated gender norms by transforming traditional "women's work" into fine art. This material repositioning is visible in works such as *Made in Western Germany*, 1987, on view in the Room 2 installation. From a distance, this untitled triptych reads like a monochromatic painting—shades of black on three panels—but, on closer inspection, it reveals its more complicated form: knitted wool pulled taut on a wood frame, revealing the repeated phrase MADE IN WESTERN GERMANY.

–CD

See Also:
Painting (55)

Truitt, Anne

b. 1921, d. 2004. Abstract artist Anne Truitt was based primarily in Washington, DC, and is often associated with male-dominated movements such as Minimalism and the Washington Color School. Truitt's practice eschewed the industrial materiality of Minimalist peers like Donald Judd; she often worked in wood, which she painted and sanded by hand. She is best known for her totemic sculptures, such as *Southern Elegy*, 1962, on view in the Room 2 installation. These works subtly engage the idea of monumentality and architecture and are inspired by natural light; their color combinations range from subdued to vibrant, playful to lyrical. Truitt was also an insightful writer; her published works, including *Daybook: The Journal of an Artist*, are eloquent meditations on what it means to live as an artist in the modern age.

–MC

See Also:
Light (82–83)
Minimal art (50)
Sculpture (65)
Wood (89–91)

Sustainability

A sustainable outlook aims to responsibly use, maintain, and fortify the resources currently available so that future generations can derive the greatest possible benefit from what they inherit. At Glenstone we broadly define "resources" to include energy, the natural environment, financial assets, archives, and art collections. We recycle, compost, use energy-efficient LED light fixtures, and source food from local farms. We have also developed in-house expertise to extend the life of institutional assets, including digital archive preservation and contemporary art conservation.
On the landscape side, extensive stream-restoration efforts are intended to revive aquatic ecosystems in the surrounding area, which have long been dormant due to erosion. Sustainability in all its forms implies a commitment to a long-term view, where progress is measured in decades, not years.

—EWR and MPR

Twombly, Cy

b. 1928, d. 2011. American artist Cy Twombly drew inspiration from multiple sources: poetry, mythology, his travels in Europe and North Africa, and a long-standing interest in symbols, which began during his time as a cryptographer for the United States military in the 1950s. Although best known for his gestural paintings incorporating scribbles, scratched lines, and words, Twombly also worked in sculpture, as evidenced by the suite of five forms currently on view in the Pavilions. Room 11 was designed in collaboration with the artist to house these particular works; most are finished in white paint or made of plaster and combine organic materials such as twine, palm leaves, and nails from Gaeta, the Italian coastal city where he lived and worked for decades.

–SW

See Also:
Assemblage (18)
Pavilions, the (83)
Plaster (84)
Sculpture (65)

Warhol, Andy

b. 1928, d. 1987. American artist, director, producer, and cultural icon Andy Warhol began his career as a commercial artist and incorporated elements from advertising and graphic design into the artwork for which he would eventually become known. Warhol was a central figure in the American Pop art movement; his silk-screened canvases, such as *Large Flowers*, 1964, on view in the Room 2 installation, are some of Pop's most recognizable images. Warhol also worked in a range of other media, producing films, television, performances, and photography, and had a penchant for entrepreneurship and collaboration, producing much of his work with teams of assistants at his infamous New York studio known as the Factory. Warhol's impresario-like activities made him a bona fide star, one who blurred the boundaries between mass culture and high art.

–JH

See Also:
Pop art (56)
Printmaking (59)

Weiner, Lawrence

b. 1942. Informed by a deep interest in sociopolitical theory and in the relationship between human beings and objects, American artist Lawrence Weiner uses language as his primary artistic material. To Weiner, words are simple, nonimposing, and malleable. By creating sculptural works out of language, Weiner offers what he defines as "a universal common possibility of availability." Evoking Minimalism's utilitarian and de-skilled ethos, Weiner's sculptures are nonprescriptive, becoming specific depending on context, installation, and reception, as such creative and interpretive decisions are left to the exhibitor and viewer. Weiner's *MATTER SO SHAKEN TO ITS CORE TO LEAD TO A CHANGE IN INHERENT FORM TO THE EXTENT OF BRINGING ABOUT A CHANGE IN THE DESTINY OF THE MATERIAL PRIMARY SECONDARY TERTIARY*, 2002, on view in the Entry Pavilion, is one of the first works visitors encounter when visiting the Pavilions.

–EB

Weiner, Lawrence

Yoshida, Toshio

b. 1928, d. 1997. Japanese artist Toshio Yoshida, perhaps the most experimental member of the Gutai group, used his work to playfully investigate the relationship between painting and performance. Chance was a large part of his practice; beginning in the 1950s, for example, Yoshida experimented by applying heat directly onto wood panels and pouring india ink onto canvas using a watering can ten feet away. *Sakuhin (56-12)*, 1956, whose title translates to "work" in English, is on view in the Room 2 installation. It is an example of Yoshida's series of "brushstroke" paintings; here, a single, enormous, thickly spread brushstroke is set against a monochromatic background. For Yoshida, such seemingly simple gestures could register as surprisingly poignant meditations on time, continuity, and presence.

–EM

See Also:
Avant-garde (19)
Gutai (39)
Painting (55)
Postwar art (58)

Architecture

At Glenstone, we aim to further the conversation about twenty-first-century museum architecture and to foster distinct architectural voices in creating unique environments for art. Our two main buildings, the Gallery and the Pavilions, which offer a total of fifty-nine thousand square feet of exhibition space, demonstrate different yet synchronous approaches to the modernist dictum "form ever follows function," and were designed expressly to support the art in Glenstone's collection. Many of the rooms in the Pavilions were developed in direct conversation with artists to house specific works of art. In other spaces, the architecture is intended to be extremely adaptable to the disparate needs of changing exhibitions.

Careful attention has been given both to the big picture—how the architecture is set into the surrounding landscape—and to the tiniest details, such as the specific color and placement of exit signage. The following pages include information about the ethos that guides our efforts, and the materials and methods that bring these buildings to life.

Climate Control

Climate control generally refers to the technology used to provide environmental comfort and to ensure healthy air quality for a building's human occupants. While heating and air-conditioning systems maintain building temperature, dehumidification systems maintain humidity levels within a desired range. Both work in conjunction with a building's ventilation system, which recirculates or replaces air to replenish oxygen and remove harmful or unpleasant airborne particulates. At Glenstone all interior climates are carefully controlled for the comfort and safety of visitors and staff and for the needs of art exhibition and storage, as proper temperature and humidification levels are essential for long-term art preservation.

—BL

See Also:
Conservation (30–31)
Ecosystem (99)
Gallery, the (78)
Green Roof (80)
LEED (81)
Pavilions, the (83)
Sustainability (71)

Concrete

Cast-in-place

The cast-in-place concrete visible in the interior of the Pavilions is a highly specialized architectural concrete, which was poured and dried on site. Its mixture includes pure white and common gray cement as well as locally quarried aggregate stones, and its formwork was handmade from Finnish plywood panels to provide a smooth and precise exterior finish. Slight natural variations are visible in its surface, including subtle changes in color, "lift lines" (from where the formwork was removed), and "bug holes" (small air pockets that formed when the cement was poured and set). These markings reflect an organic process that produces an elegant and idiosyncratic material; no two panels are ever fully alike.

—VN

See Also:
Pavilions, the (83)

Precast

The light gray facade and interior walls of the Pavilions are made up of approximately twenty-six thousand precast concrete blocks, each measuring six feet by one foot in length. These blocks were poured off-site and cast from the same mixture and formwork. While uniform, each block is also unique: weather conditions during the casting and curing process have resulted in a spectrum of color variations—blocks poured in the winter darkened due to colder temperatures and a slower evaporation of water, and blocks stripped (i.e., removed from their formwork) in the rain developed a higher contrast in surface finish than those that were stripped in sunlight. The exterior blocks of the Pavilions are stacked up to sixty feet high, and their surfaces will develop further contrast over time as the material ages and weathers.

—VN

See Also:
Pavilions, the (83)
Phifer, Thomas (84)

Concrete

Entrance

The journey to Glenstone begins along Glen Road, where a stretch of reforested terrain recalls the area's original woodlands. As visitors turn off the road to enter, they pass through an entry gate of dry-laid stone, made of Carderock quarried nearby. Built according to centuries-old tradition and partly inspired by Andy Goldsworthy's outdoor sculpture *Clay Houses (Boulder-Room-Holes)*, 2007, the stone entry wall embodies the same architectural principles as the Pavilions, employing simple materials in precise ways. The journey continues to the parking groves (each planted with a tree species native to the surrounding forest), past the arrival hall, over a small footbridge, and out into a sprawling meadow, where a visitor's first glimpse of the Pavilions is framed by a large American sycamore and Jeff Koons's *Split-Rocker*, 2000, in the distance. The entry sequence is orchestrated to encourage visitors to slow down and take a breath, and to fuel a sense of curiosity about what lies ahead.

—FG

Framed Views

In East Asian garden design, "borrowed scenery" (借景) is a technique of incorporating views of distant landmarks into a garden composition. Architect Thomas Phifer's concept for the Pavilions was in part inspired by the dry garden at Ryōan-ji, the Buddhist temple in Kyoto that employs framed views to great effect. The garden features fifteen stones placed asymmetrically within a rectangular field of raked gravel. From the adjacent platform, there is no single vantage point that permits a complete view of all fifteen stones, which has led some to interpret the garden as a Zen koan—a meditation strategy used by monks to suspend reason in favor of intuition. Likewise, it is impossible to see all twelve structures that comprise the Pavilions from the surrounding landscape. The undulating topography and sinuous pathways leading to the entrance work in concert to gradually reveal the massing of architectural forms as visitors traverse the landscape.

—EWR

See Also:
Pavilions, the (83)

Gallery, The

The Gallery opened to the public in 2006 as Glenstone's first architectural space for art. The building was designed, along with the adjacent Patio, by New York–based architect Charles Gwathmey. Gwathmey envisioned the Gallery as providing two very different, extremely flexible situations for displaying art: a gallery flooded with natural light (the space one enters from the outside), and interior rooms that provide a more traditional "white cube" environment, separated from the outdoors. Speaking about the project in 2005, Gwathmey championed its integration of the spheres of art and architecture: "I think that's really what makes this so enriched and unique . . . the art and the architecture are not disengaged and are not incompatible philosophically. They're mutually engaged, and make a much more dynamic experience."

—EB

See Also:
Exhibition (34)
Gwathmey, Charles (81)
Light (82–83)
Pond (104)
Sight line (105)

Framed views

Glass

Acid-etched

Acid-etched glass is created by washing clear glass in a light acid bath to create a uniform and semitransparent glazing (a technique that produces a smoother finish than sandblasting, in which high-pressure air is used to cut the glass surface). A type of glass etching—itself a popular decorative technique—acid-etching allows bright yet diffused light to penetrate from the outside world in. The clerestories in the Pavilions are made of acid-etched glass, offering a particularly even light for the display of art.

–VN

See Also:
Clerestory (82)
Conservation (30–31)
Light (82–83)

Transparent

Dozens of large, seamless transparent glass panels line the eighteen-thousand-square-foot Water Court at the center of the Pavilions. Measuring up to thirty feet tall and set in stainless-steel mullions, these German-made panels—some of the largest in the world—open a dialogue between the interior and exterior, connecting the exhibition spaces with the landscape. The largest glass panel in the Pavilions is the window in Room 7; engineered specifically for the space, the window faces acres of rolling meadow, offering viewers a moment of repose.

–EM

See Also:
Framed views (78–79)
Horn, Roni (40)
Sight line (105)
Water Court (88)

Green Roof

A primary design consideration for the Pavilions centered on Glenstone's mission statement: to seamlessly integrate art, architecture, and the landscape. By physically embedding portions of the two-acre building into the earth, with nearly 50 percent of its surface covered in soil and native flowers and grasses, the Pavilions have a "green roof" that provides numerous environmental and structural benefits. In addition to improved storm-water management from reduced runoff, our green roof improves water quality, conserves energy, mitigates the urban "heat island" effect, increases the longevity of roofing membranes, reduces noise and air pollution, sequesters carbon in the soil, and provides habitat for wildlife.

–PT

See Also:
Ecosystem (99)
LEED (81)
Pavilions, the (83)
Storm-water management (107–108)
Sustainability (71)

Gwathmey, Charles

b. 1938, d. 2009. Charles Gwathmey was one of the preeminent modernist architects of the generation that came of age in the 1960s and 1970s. Educated at the University of Pennsylvania and Yale, he achieved recognition early in his career for the house and studio he designed in Amagansett, New York, in 1965 for his parents, the painter Robert Gwathmey and the photographer Rosalie Gwathmey. A pair of stark wooden structures of powerful and simple geometries, the Gwathmey house and studio were widely publicized and influenced a generation of modernist houses; the structures are now considered among the iconic American residences of the mid-twentieth century. Along with his partner Robert Siegel, Gwathmey went on to design a wide range of commercial and institutional buildings, including the Gallery at Glenstone, but unlike many architects with large and varied practices, designing houses remained his passion. Even as his work became both more elaborate and more complex, he continued to explore the themes of modernist space and form—often influenced by the work of Le Corbusier—that had inspired his parents' home and studio. His oeuvre includes numerous large modernist residences in California, Texas, and Europe, as well as a residence and guest house on the Glenstone property that reinterpret the traditional villa, at once celebrations of grandeur and expressions of intricate modernist geometries.

–PG

See Also:
Gallery, the (8–9, 78)
Oculus (83)
Teak (95)
Zinc (91)

LEED

Leadership in Energy and Environmental Design (LEED) is a worldwide rating system used to certify green buildings based on principles of design, construction, operation, and maintenance. At Glenstone, all architectural projects aim to maximize efficiency of resources, reduce emissions, and keep costs down—a process that involves careful selection of construction materials, fixtures, and the implementation of building management systems that monitor energy output for optimal use. LEED offers four levels of certification: Certified, Silver, Gold, and Platinum; different buildings at Glenstone have been designed with different certification levels in mind, ranging from Gold (the Pavilions) to Platinum (Arrival Hall).

–CJ

See Also:
Climate control (76)
Green roof (80)
LED (82)
Pavilions, the (83)
Sustainability (71)

Light

Clerestory

Middle English for "clear story," the term *clerestory* was originally used to reference the narrow upper-level windows placed at the highest section of a wall to admit air and light into a church or cathedral. At Glenstone, the clerestory windows provide soft, natural light in the Pavilions, which changes throughout the day and seasons.

–VN

See Also:
Acid-etched glass (80)
Pavilions, the (83)
Phifer, Thomas (84)

LED

LEDs (light-emitting diodes) are the primary type of artificial lighting used at Glenstone, meant to augment the abundant natural light in the museum's buildings. LEDs have many advantages over incandescent light sources, including lower energy consumption (at least 75 percent less), better longevity (with LEDs lasting approximately twenty-five times longer), improved physical robustness, and smaller size. They offer better light quality and repeatable dimming, both of which are important for use in a museum. LEDs are capable of emitting directional light, which reduces the amount of light required and eliminates the need for reflectors and diffusers. Because less heat is produced by LEDs, the cooling load on the building is reduced in turn—for every three kilowatt hours of energy saved by using lower-energy LEDs, around another one kilowatt hour of energy is saved by the building's cooling system.

–CJ

See Also:
Climate control (76)

Louver

Louvers are angled or flat slats used to control the flow of air and/or light in architectural settings. At Glenstone, louvers are used as environmental controls. In the Gallery, louvers facilitate the amount of natural light that can enter the space, providing control over how light may affect art objects on display. When fully open, the louvers in the Gallery's skylight allow for the maximum amount of available natural light; conversely, closed louvers are more appropriate for displaying works requiring the consistency of artificial light, or which are—like color photography—sensitive to prolonged sun exposure.

–JH

See Also:
Gallery, the (78)

Pavilions, The

The Pavilions were conceived as a gathering of rooms encircling a central water court, thoughtfully embedded in the surrounding landscape. From a distance, these rooms appear as a cluster rising from the meadow, recalling the medieval town of San Gimignano (known as the "town of fine towers"), a touchstone when developing the Pavilions' plan. Each room was designed with unique proportions; many were designed expressly for specific works of art. The building's primary materials are concrete and glass, blending a sense of permanence and of the ethereal. Natural light is considered here as a material in its own right: rooms were placed deliberately on the cardinal points in order to highlight the movement of the sun's daily passage, and many are intended to be lit by natural light alone. In moving through the various rooms and the glass-enclosed circulation path, light seems to dissolve the barrier between outside and inside, between landscape and architecture.

–TPP

Oculus

An oculus (from the Latin word meaning "eye") is a circular or oval opening, usually at the center of a dome, through which light or precipitation may pass, and which often served historically as a building's ventilation system. The oculus as architectural feature has its origins in ancient Rome, where perhaps one of the most famous examples of the form, the central aperture in the Pantheon, can still be seen today. Charles Gwathmey incorporated an oculus at the entrance of Glenstone's Gallery, though not in the traditional context: the oculus pierces the zinc overhang, mirroring the opening at the top of Richard Serra's nearby *Sylvester*, 2001. Visitors to the museum have often noted the similarity when looking up through the oculus and through Sylvester: the sky seems to become part of both the art and architecture.

–SE

See Also:
Gallery, the (78)
Gwathmey, Charles (81)

Shade

The shade system in the Pavilions is an integral element of the building's lighting design, with large shades installed to cover the windows in the Passage and the clerestories in several rooms. These shades are controlled by sensors that automatically adjust to changing daylight exposures; when these sensors detect too much heat or sunlight, the shades automatically lower to block additional light, and when they register a dimming of light, they trigger the reverse. In regulating light and heat retention, shades supplement Glenstone's art conservation efforts in significant ways, by both reducing art's exposure to harmful amounts of light, and ensuring desirable climate control within the gallery spaces.

–EB

Phifer, Thomas

b. 1953. Thomas Phifer, the architect of the Pavilions at Glenstone, was awarded the commission in late 2010 after a two-stage invitational competition, for which he proposed a museum of multiple pavilions, unequal in size, arrayed around a central reflecting pool. Unlike many designs submitted to architectural competitions, Phifer's project was built largely as he had initially conceived it. Prior to Glenstone, Phifer designed the North Carolina Museum of Art in Raleigh and the expansion of the Corning Museum of Glass in Corning, New York. Phifer—who worked early in his career for Charles Gwathmey, the architect of the Gallery at Glenstone, and later with Richard Meier—established his own practice in New York in 1997. His most notable early commission was not a building, but a design for a new, sensuously curved LED street lamp for New York City. Although the Pavilions at Glenstone are primarily masonry structures intended to sit like solid objects in the landscape, Phifer is best known for works that are exceptionally light, almost weightless in appearance. All of his work shares a meticulous, highly refined sense of detailing and an unusual grace.

—PG

See Also:
Light (82–83)
Framed views (78–79)
Pavilions, the (83)
Water Court (88)

Plaster

Used as both a protective and decorative coating, plaster is a type of wall treatment applied directly onto a raw substrate in successive layers. Its use can be traced as far back as ancient Pompeiian and Roman structures, and it continues to be commonly employed in construction today. The plaster in the Pavilions is made entirely from natural minerals, including a lime paste composed of rocks from the Ticino River (which flows from Switzerland through Northern Italy) and Italian marble dust.

—EB and VN

See Also:
Bourgeois, Louise (22–23)
Oldenburg, Claes (54)
Pavilions, the (83)
Twombly, Cy (72)

Community

At Glenstone we believe that the arts are essential to a just and humane society. The arts can serve as a shared language that bridges differences in culture, class, or ideology. Art is also an invitation to dream—to lose oneself in an aesthetic experience. Through our program with Montgomery County Public Schools, we have hosted more than five thousand students from grades four through twelve, many of whom had never visited an art museum before coming to Glenstone. In keeping with our commitment to arts integration, we conduct extensive outreach and develop programming not only with arts organizations, but also maker spaces, community colleges, lifelong learning centers, professional associations, and hospitals throughout the Capital region.

–EWR and MPR

Stainless Steel

Popularized in the early twentieth century, stainless steel is a steel alloy incorporating chromium and other elements, which create a corrosion-resistant barrier that protects the surface from damage. Stainless steel is used extensively at Glenstone for its elegance and durability. In contemplating the Pavilions' design in particular, the Glenstone team discussed various grades and lusters of steel, and debated percentages of nickel, chromium, and manganese, ultimately settling on basic stainless steel for its unparalleled longevity and its elemental beauty.

–TCe

See Also:
Kelly, Ellsworth (44)
Ray, Charles (62)
Pavilions, the (83)

Stone

Argillite

Argillite refers to a type of sedimentary rock composed of hardened clay particles, with color and composition varying depending on region. The argillite installed around Michael Heizer's *Compression Line*, 1968/2016, and *Collapse*, 1967/2016, in and outside the Pavilions, was mined in the southwest United States. The artist chose this specific type of argillite for its color: the reddish-brown rock resembles the rusted patina of the weathering-steel sculptures, heightening a contrast in texture while creating a feeling of expansiveness in their final installation. The use of this particular argillite is also practical: it produces minimal dust and does not crumble—or crunch—when walked on, furthering the sculptures' sense of quiet solidity.

–MLe

See Also:
Heizer, Michael (40)

Carderock

Carderock is a mica-schist quartzite stone native to Montgomery County, Maryland, and, along with Glen Road (the "Glen"), inspired the name "Glenstone." The stone is incorporated throughout the museum's art, architecture, and landscape: Andy Goldsworthy, known for working closely with nature and local materials, chose Carderock for the outdoor sculpture *Clay Houses (Boulder-Room-Holes)*, 2007; Glenstone's entrance wall is made of Carderock, as are the steps embedded in the landscape leading to the bridle trail; and in the parking groves, large slabs of Carderock designate individual spaces. The multifaceted use of this indigenous stone both highlights the native landscape and demonstrates Glenstone's commitment to coherent integration.

–TCe and KB

See Also:
Entrance (78)
Goldsworthy, Andy (36–37)
Stream restoration (108)

Stone

Granite

Granite is a durable igneous rock made of feldspar, mica, and quartz, whose name derives from its visible grains (the Latin word for grain is *granum*). Granite has been used as both a sculptural and architectural material for centuries, utilized in the creations of civilizations dating as far back as ancient Egypt. The most prominent use of granite at Glenstone is in the Gallery, where it is used for the building's exterior cladding; it is also used for the pavers on which Richard Serra's *Sylvester*, 2001, and Felix Gonzalez-Torres's *Untitled*, 1992–1995, rest. In the Pavilions, granite also lines the edge of the Water Court.

–TG

See Also:
Gallery, the (78)
Water Court (88)

Terrazzo

A durable composite building material comprised of stone chips set in a binder, such as concrete or epoxy, and then honed and polished for a smooth finish. Typically fashioned with marble or granite—Glenstone's terrazzo is marble—terrazzo is often used for slab-construction flooring. Favored by modern architects such as Richard Neutra, Frank Lloyd Wright, and Charles Gwathmey, terrazzo is employed in the Pavilions to complement the building's concrete and glass. The Pavilion's terrazzo is unique in several ways: it was designed and installed using minimal expansion joints, or stainless-steel strips used to control shifting; it is an unusually light color, with very small aggregate; and it has been polished to a matte finish, rather than a high-gloss, glass-like finish, as is more typical.

–LL

See Also:
Pavilions, the (83)
Phifer, Thomas (84)

Water Court

The Water Court is the central courtyard within the Pavilions, accessible by a single outdoor viewing platform outside of Room 6. Lowered into the topography and surrounded by architecture, the Court fully reveals itself only when viewers first descend the building's main staircase. Growth, bloom, and decay are visible at close range, and reflections of the sky, dragonflies in flight, wind, weather, and time all register within its borders. While this garden may look composed, the plant species spread and colonize new locations as they acclimate to the particular conditions found within the glass enclosure. The Water Court anchors the experience of visitors as they move between each of the rooms in the Pavilions, cycling from art to architecture to landscape, again and again.

–AG

See Also:
Aquatics (94–95)
Framed views (79–80)
Ipe (90)
Pavilions, the (83)
Peter Walker and Partners (104)

Wood

Alaskan Yellow Cedar

Alaskan yellow cedar clads the exterior of the Arrival Hall, the Café, and the rails of the pedestrian bridges. It was the wood of choice because when it "silvers," or gently grays with age, it takes on a hue similar to the gray of the Pavilions' precast concrete blocks. Even though Alaskan yellow cedar has the rich aroma that cedars are known for (similar to raw potatoes) and bears the cedar name, it is in fact a variety of cypress tree. Alaskan yellow cedar is a softwood, and is not used on surfaces that bear foot or vehicular traffic.

–LL

See Also:
Entrance (78)
Pavilions, the (83)
Phifer, Thomas (84)

Ash

While terrazzo is the flooring material used for the viewing galleries in the Pavilions, there is one notable exception: Room 3, where artist On Kawara specifically requested a wooden floor for the space that would hold his painting trilogy, *Moon Landing*, 1969. In collaboration with the architect and Kawara's estate, Glenstone worked to select and source a light, wide-planed ash for this purpose—a hardwood known for being strong yet flexible, and often used in making bows, guitars, and baseball bats. The change in materials marks a subtle shift as visitors cross the threshold into this room—the tallest in the Pavilions, and one of the last projects the artist oversaw personally before his death in 2014.

–AR and VN

See Also:
Kawara, On (44)

Douglas Fir

Reaching an average mature height of over three hundred feet, Douglas fir is considered one of the strongest timbers grown in the Americas. Due to its durability, natural color variations, and resistance to decay, Douglas fir bark has been used for flooring in factories and warehouses since the nineteenth century, as a support for heavy industrial material and machinery. In the Gallery, the exhibition flooring consists of a mosaic of multicolored and multi-textured Douglas fir pieces, which were laid by hand. In choosing this particular wood for the space, architect Charles Gwathmey explained that the flooring should "always be archaeological. It'll show the marks of where the other exhibition walls used to be and [it will] develop its own patina . . . [becoming] part of the story."

–KB

See Also:
Gallery, the (78)
Gwathmey, Charles (81)

Hickory

An open-grain, fast-growing, porous wood, hickory bends easily yet is challenging to work by hand and to machine. Known especially for its resiliency, woodworkers often choose hickory for materials and tools that require heavy use, such as wagon wheels, skis, and hammer handles. Hickory is extremely durable and utilitarian, but more difficult to use than similar woods (such as maple) due to its tough composition. The base of the monumental bench in the Viewing Gallery (Room 7 in the Pavilions) is made of hickory.

–NSC

See Also:
Puryear, Martin (60–61)

Ipe

Ipe, native to Central and South America, is often referred to as a Brazilian walnut. Ipe's durability, longevity, and resistance to insects makes it a good choice for exterior use, and if left unstained the surface will weather to a silver gray. Though dense and at times hard to cut or nail into, ipe is known for its range of rich colors and its environmental friendliness, as it does not need to be replaced often. At Glenstone ipe is used in the Water Court platform, the Patio deck, the Boardwalk, and the bridges.

–KB

See Also:
Water Court (88)

Maple

A relatively inexpensive wood, maple is plentiful across the United States and characterized by its light color and closed pores. The diverse materiality of this wood lends itself to use in products as varied as musical instruments—like the violin—and recreational equipment such as bowling pins. Its use at Glenstone is also diverse: the Viewing Gallery (Room 7 in the Pavilions) is entirely clad in maple, as are the interiors of the Café and Arrival Hall. The top portion of the eighteen-foot-long Viewing Gallery bench is made of maple as well.

–NSC

See Also:
Pavilions, the (83)
Puryear, Martin (60–61)

Zinc

Teak

Originally from the South Asian rainforest, teak has a deep golden-brown color that, when left unsealed, weathers to a silver-gray patina. Long favored as a boat-building and decking material due to its durability and resistance to moisture, teak grew in popularity in the United States and Europe as a residential building material during the middle of the twentieth century, and is thus particularly associated with mid-century modern style. At Glenstone, teak is used both in the Gallery and the Water Court bench in the Pavilions.

–KB

See Also:
Pond (104)
Water Court (88)

A chemical element found in the earth's crust, zinc is mined and smelted for use as an industrial material. Due to its abundance and affordability, zinc was a popular material for sculpture—especially statuary—in the 1800s; as a sculptural material it requires little maintenance and develops a distinct matte patina over time. Today it is often used in architecture, as its lightness and malleability can accommodate curves and other complex shapes. At Glenstone zinc can be seen as cladding on a portion of the Gallery's exterior, where its surface gently contrasts with the building's gray granite shell. Architect Charles Gwathmey selected zinc for this particular use, he said, for its "groundedness."

–SE

See Also:
Gallery, the (78)
Water Court (88)

Landscape

Glenstone sits on approximately 230 acres of land in the Potomac River Valley, land that includes rolling hills, active streams, perennial meadows, and woodland pathways with mature specimen trees. The site is entirely maintained via organic means and methods, practices that support a wide range of local ecosystems, flora, and fauna.

Our approach to landscape design privileges the restoration of natural systems, and aims to create a balance between these systems and the museum's manmade environments. Outdoor artworks are placed with special care and attention. The following pages provide a snapshot of various design features and principles that anchor Glenstone's outdoor spaces, a description of processes used to develop and maintain the site, and commentary on a selection of plants and animals that you might encounter during a visit.

Aquatics

Marliac White Water Lily
Nymphaea 'Marliacea albida'

Of the nearly five hundred water lilies planted in the Water Court at the center of the Pavilions, a large majority are *Nymphaea Marliacea albida*, named for the French horticulturist Joseph Bory Latour-Marliac, who first hybridized the lily in 1880. Latour-Marliac supplied Claude Monet with lilies for his pond in Giverny, France, which became the subject of some of his most famous Impressionist paintings. The 'Marliacea albida' leaf spread spans twelve square feet and freely blooms from May to October, with each blossom lasting approximately three days. This aquatic flower brings balance to the Water Court's aquatic ecosystem, absorbing nutrients and blocking harmful UV rays.

—JSa

See Also:
Water Court (88)

Clockwise, from top right:
graceful cattail (*Typha laxmannii*), Texas dawn (*Nympahea*), purple thalia (*Thalia dealbata*), pickerel rush (*Pontederia cordata*), Louisiana iris 'Count Pulaski,' blue flag (*Iris versicolor*), common rush (*Juncus effusus*)

Birds

Clockwise, from top right:
ringed-necked pheasant (*Phaisanus colchicus*), red-shouldered hawk (*Buteo lineatus*),
northern mockingbird (*Mimus polyglottos*), red-bellied woodpecker (*Melanerpes carolinus*),
turkey vulture (*Cathartes aura*), red-winged blackbird (*Agelaius phoeniceus*), northern
cardinal (*Cardinalis cardinalis*), tree swallow (*Tachycineta bicolor*)

Clockwise, from top right:
double-crested cormorant (*Phalacrocorax auritus*), blue jay (*Cyanocitta cristata*),
American robin (*Turdus migratorius*), Canada goose (*Branta canadensis*),
dark-eyed junco (*Junco hyemalis*), killdeer (*Charadrius vociferus*), barred owl (*Strix varia*),
American crow (*Corvus brachyrhynchos*)

Great Blue Heron
Ardea herodias

The dignified great blue heron (*Ardea herodias*) is found throughout North America, often along bodies of water. This heron is the largest of its species, and resides farther north than others, even during winter months when waters freeze. The great blue heron frequently spotted at Glenstone, nicknamed "the Admiral," can be seen effortlessly gliding over the landscape before landing along the banks of the Gallery Pond. Standing guard over the water, as still as the cattails, visitors may see the Admiral waiting for the opportune time to dive into the pond to catch an unsuspecting fish.

–ST

See Also:
Ecosystem (99)
Pond (104)
Wildlife (114–115)

Ecosystem

An ecosystem is a community of organisms—insects, plants, animals, and humans—living in a specific environment. Each member of this complex system has a specific purpose, and when a member is removed—or when an invasive species is introduced—the whole community is affected. Glenstone's ecosystem is wide and diverse, consisting of meadows, woodlands, ponds, and streams rich in local flora, which in turn supports native fauna. Beneficial bugs and plants are introduced to the ecosystem when needed, supporting this balance. Visitors are encouraged to explore the mini-ecosystems throughout the landscape, from the fish and birds in the Gallery Pond to the trees and understories along the Woodland Trail.

–MR

See Also:
Community (85)
Meadow (103)
Pond (104)
Reforestation (105)
Soil (105–106)
Stream restoration (108)

Environmental Center

A dynamic living classroom that changes daily, the Environmental Center at Glenstone is a multiuse maintenance and education facility offering hands-on, experiential learning. Served by its own entrance at the northwest corner of the campus on Glen Road, the Environmental Center houses world-class landscape and educational teams, which welcome the opportunity to share Glenstone's all-organic techniques and discoveries with visitors. Included among the many take-home ideas are on-site composting and compost-tea brewing, natural landscape management, waste reduction, materials recycling, and water conservation. Though tours and classes may be scheduled in advance, informal drop-ins are welcome.

–PT

See Also:
Compost tea (106)
Horticulture (103)
Sustainability (71)

Farm and Forage

The phrase *farm and forage* refers to a principle of sustainability—one that informs how ingredients for Glenstone's cafés are sourced. Like its close cousin "farm to table," the farm-and-forage ethos prioritizes on-site farming, beekeeping, and partnering with nearby farmers. To these standards it adds the practice of foraging from local land. Farm and forage is also about tasting place, experiencing the landscape and locality through flavor and nourishment. While Glenstone's food program is in its early stages of development, the intention is ultimately to incorporate ingredients foraged from the woods and meadows on-site into offerings at both of Glenstone's cafés—such as the native pawpaw fruit and local nuts and berries.

–MLo and BP

See Also:
Horticulture (103)
Sustainability (71)
Woodlands (116)

100 Flowers   Landscape

Flowers

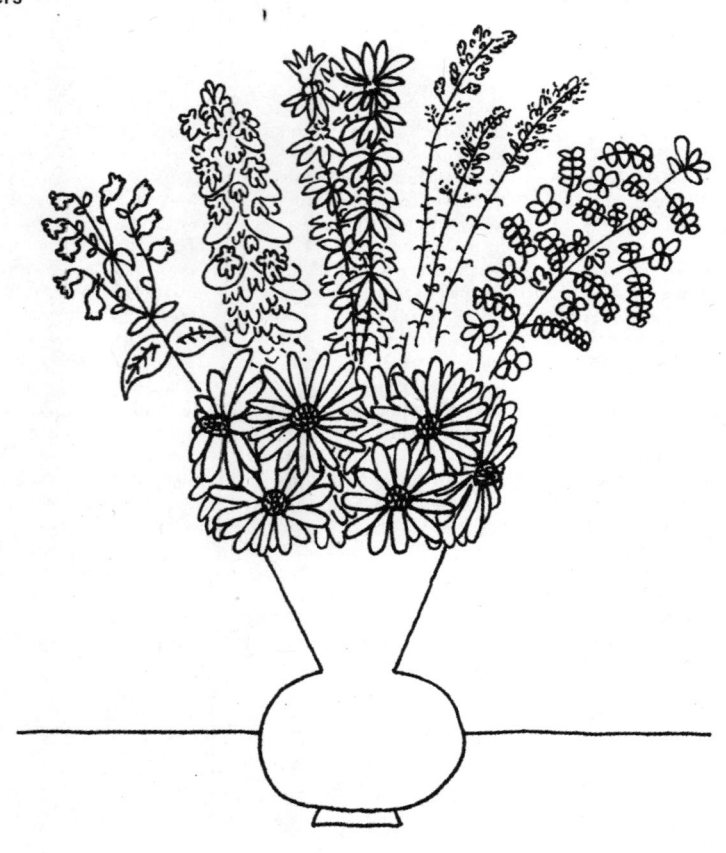

Clockwise from top left:
beardtongue (*Penstemon digitalis*), bugleweed (*Ajuga reptans*),
dotted horsemint (*Monarda punctata*), grey goldenrod (*Solidago nemoralis*),
partridge pea (*Chamaecrista fasciculata*), black-eyed Susan (*Rudbeckia hirta*)

Clockwise from top left:
golden Alexander (*Zizia aureua*), zinnia (*Zinnia elegans*),
swamp milkweed (*Asclepias incarnate*), Petchoa 'SuperCal Blue,'
French marigold (*Tagetes patula*)

New Guinea Impatiens
Impatiens hawkeri

New Guinea impatiens (*Impatiens hawkeri*) is a species of flowering plant native to New Guinea and the Solomon Islands, with flowers that bloom from spring to early fall. The New Guinea impatiens has a wide variety of petal colors, and prefers partial shade and well-drained soils. This species is generally hearty, and not prone to disease or insect infestation. All these characteristics make the New Guinea impatiens perfect for Jeff Koons's *Split-Rocker*, 2000, which is planted each year with thousands of flowers that are then organically maintained. Different varieties of this flower are used on both sides of *Split-Rocker*: a more sun-tolerant variety for Dino and one that prefers shade for Pony.

—CR

See Also:
Koons, Jeff (46)
Horticulture (103)
Mosiaculture (104)

Forest Bathing

The phrase *forest bathing* derives from the Japanese word *shinrin-yoku*, referring to a health-and-wellness practice developed in Japan in the early 1980s. Its ethos extends an intuitive human supposition and experience; namely, that time in nature can prove restful and ultimately restorative. *Shinrin-yoku* encourages relaxed and meditative walks outdoors, and the practice is congruent with Glenstone's desire to create a serene and contemplative environment for visitors as well as its emphasis on landscape and nature as aesthetic experiences. As famed naturalist, philosopher, and author Henry David Thoreau once wrote of his beloved Walden: "We need the tonic of wildness . . . we can never have enough nature."

—FG and AR

See Also:
Woodlands (116)
Cardiff, Janet and George Bures Miller (26–27)

Horticulture

Horticulture is a specific facet of agriculture that focuses on the individual care of plants, blending both the science of growing and the art of design. There are tens of thousands of new trees, flowers, and understories at Glenstone, all selected and planted according to sustainable practices in landscape design. A team of Glenstone horticulturists nurtures these plants to unify the landscaped and natural areas, prunes newly established trees for health and structure, and identifies and organically eliminates invasive weeds in the acres of native meadows.

—MP

See Also:
Meadow (103)
New Guinea impatiens (102)
Pond (104)
Soil (105–106)
Woodlands (116)

Meadow

Meadows are typically composed of grasslands and wildflowers, and form a unique ecosystem. Glenstone's nearly forty acres of meadow provide one of the anchoring foundations of the landscape, guiding visitors toward the Pavilions and the Gallery, and offering multiple vistas along the way. The native grasses that were chosen specifically for this site will mature at approximately three feet in height and nurture a balanced ecosystem while emphasizing the contours of the restored terrain. Conceived as a long-term project, the meadow allows nature to take its course, creating new plant and wildlife combinations annually.

—MP

See Also:
Little bluestem (112)
Koons, Jeff (46)
Serra, Richard (65)

Mosaiculture

Mosaiculture is the hortcultural practice of using multiple plants to create a living, three-dimensional composition. At Glenstone the outdoor sculpture *Split-Rocker*, 2000, by Jeff Koons, offers a monumental example of this practice. Approximately twenty-two thousand annuals are planted on *Split-Rocker* each spring, including over a dozen species of brightly colored flowers. Supporting this floral ecosystem is a hollow stainless-steel structure, the outer layer of which is filled with a custom mix of organic soils, carefully calibrated to ensure proper conditions for plant growth. *Split-Rocker* has an internal irrigation system that delivers water, natural fertilizers (such as compost tea), and natural fungicides, which are all vital for sustaining this living sculpture. *Split-Rocker* is the first work of art visitors encounter when approaching the Pavilions and embodies the integration of art, architecture, and landscape so central to Glenstone's mission.

—CR

See Also:
Koons, Jeff (46)
New Guinea impatiens (102)

Peter Walker and Partners

Based in San Francisco, PWP Landscape Architects, or Peter Walker and Partners, have worked in close collaboration with artists and architects to define Glenstone's landscape design since the museum's inception more than a decade ago. Internationally renowned for their thoughtful approach to public spaces (past projects include the Nasher Sculpture Center in Dallas and the plaza for the National September 11 Memorial in New York), PWP's work is often characterized by a modernist approach, a refined simplicity, and a close attention to material selection and craft. Their overall site plan at Glenstone is an ongoing, long-term project that aims to integrate all aspects of the site's diverse landscape into a cohesive whole, and to enrich the relationship between Glenstone's natural environment, its architecture, and outdoor works of art.

—EWR

See Also:
Commission (28)
Framed views (78–79)
Sight line (105)
Sustainability (71)

Pond

The aquatic ecosystems at Glenstone feature three ponds: the Gallery pond, the Water Court, and the Lily Pond. The Gallery pond is the largest, at nearly three acres, and ranges from four to fourteen feet deep; it is bordered by a diverse bed of irises and cattails, and frogs, fish, and freshwater clams are abundant, frequently attracting birds. The Water Court, planted with a variety of waterlilies, irises, rushes, cattails, and hardy canna, is the centerpiece of the Pavilions, featuring seventeen thousand square feet of water. Naturally balanced and sustainable, the Water Court is organically maintained and supported by a state-of-the-art filtration system. The Lily Pond is the oldest and smallest pond, dating back to when the land was first established as grounds for a fox-hunting club in the 1940s. The surface is covered in yellow pond lily (*Nuphar lutea*), a waterlily that dawns canary yellow blossoms, and the muddy banks are densely planted with lizard's tail (*Saururus cernuus*) and water iris.

—JSa

Reforestation

Reforestation refers to the replanting of trees, "understory" vegetation such as shrubs, and groundcover flora on sites where previous plant life has been lost. Glenstone, which is sited on more than two hundred acres of land, has prioritized reforestation for many years—during its expansion from 2013 to 2018 the team installed more than seven thousand trees, tens of thousands of shrubs, and millions of annual and perennial grasses and flowers. Although some ornamental plants remain on site from an earlier era on the property, Glenstone now plants only native, regionally appropriate species, which require the fewest resources to maintain and provide appropriate food and habitat for local fauna. Glenstone also partners closely with Montgomery County in ensuring that its acres of forested land will be protected through optimal conservation practices.

–PT

See Also:
Community (85)
Conservation (30–31)
Forest Bathing (103)
Sustainability (71)

Sight Line

A sight line is the implied course from a viewer's eye to the object of vision. Glenstone pays close attention to sight lines in order to enhance the experience of its landscape, architecture, and outdoor works of art. Siting paths and gathering spaces within a valley surrounded by trees keeps sight lines shorter and creates a feeling of intimacy. Clearing out obstructions from a particular location to the horizon extends views dramatically into the distance. Focal points are situated in a variety of ways: sunken into the topography, nestled in the woods, or set on a hill. Specific pieces of art and architecture are also sited with attention to sight lines—either kept from view to facilitate an impactful reveal, as when the Water Court becomes fully visible on descending from the Entry Pavilion to the Passage, or set high at a significant distance, such as *Split-Rocker*, 2000, which becomes a beacon pulling visitors onward through the landscape.

–AG

See Also:
Entrance (78)

Soil

Soil is a mixture composed principally of sand, silt, clay, organic matter, water, and air. Two main types of soil are found at Glenstone: native and custom-blend. The native soil is mostly silt loam, which contains a high percentage of clay and silt; this varietal was used by Andy Goldsworthy in creating the work *Clay Houses (Boulder-Room-Holes)*, 2007. A custom-blended structural soil was used in building the parking groves; it includes a large percentage of sand to prevent compaction and allow for faster drainage during periods of heavy rain. A special soil is also used in Jeff Koons's *Split-Rocker*, 2000, containing organic ingredients and designed to drain easily, retain moisture, and last for several years before needing to be replaced.

–CR

See Also:
Beuys, Joseph (20–21)
Goldsworthy, Andy (36–37)
Green roof (80)

Aeration

The health of any landscape depends on its soil. In general, Glenstone can control water, air, and organic matter by "feeding" the soils with compost and natural fertilizers to maintain organic matter, supplying water as needed, and facilitating aeration in areas that have become overly compacted and can't "breathe." This is typically accomplished with a specialized machine—an aerator—that cuts soil plugs out of the ground, thereby creating a network of holes where air, water, and nutrients can readily enter into the root structure.

–PT

See Also:
Meadow (103)

Compost tea

Compost tea is composted material soaked in water—a safe and sustainable mixture that facilitates optimal plant growth and health. Glenstone deploys an advanced system to make its compost tea, using a process that involves approximately thirty hours of "steeping," along with constant agitation and oxygenation. During the steeping, nutrients and biological elements from the solid compost are dissolved into the water, and the resulting "tea," a dark brown liquid, functions as both a fertilizer and soil amendment. It is either sprayed or applied via irrigation systems, and depending on the needs of the plants—lawns and trees vary in their requirements—the compost tea can be modified accordingly.

–PT

See Also:
Environmental Center (99)

Nitrogen cycle/fixation

Plants need an abundance of nutrients to thrive, the most important of which is typically nitrogen. Though this element is abundant in the air we breathe—air is about 79 percent nitrogen gas—it remains inaccessible to most plant types. The exceptions are legumes, which can store, or "fix," nitrogen. The most prominent example of a legume at Glenstone is clover; the roots of this flowering plant contain rhizobium bacteria, which live in small nodules in the clover's root system. When the nodules break off into the soil, the nitrogen is released, or "cycled," so that grass and other plants can absorb the nitrogen they need—a truly symbiotic relationship.

–PT

See Also:
Meadow (103)
Woodlands (116)

Storm-Water Management

Glenstone sits on a vast sloping site surrounded by stream valleys and wetlands. The museum's landscape architects, civil engineers, and grounds team members have developed and implemented a comprehensive system to manage rainfall flow throughout the property. This process involves planting trees, shrubs, and understory plants appropriate to the region, as well as the construction of underground drainage systems designed to direct water flow into specific areas, including three underground cisterns and three surface ponds. In instances when storm water does reach the lowest points of the site—the floodplains—all natural inlets have been fortified with step pools reinforced by holding walls constructed from logs and boulders, to eliminate any sediment from entering the streams, thereby protecting insect and aquatic life.

–PT

See Also:
Cistern (107)
Ecosystem (99)
Little bluestem (112)
Pond (104)
Sustainability (71)

Bioretention areas

Wherever there are large areas of impermeable paving, storm-water runoff can have significant negative environmental and structural impact. Glenstone has mitigated any chance of storm-water damage through the construction of contoured areas in the landscape that intentionally collect and absorb excess water. These bioretention bogs, wetlands, and ponds are planted with native plant species that naturally withstand extremely moist conditions, as well as the occasional droughts experienced in the mid-Atlantic region. These areas are havens for insects and other fauna, and are among the most biologically diverse places on the Glenstone site.

–PT

See Also:
Ecosystem (99)
Peter Walker and Partners (104)

Cistern

Recognizing that water for irrigation is essential in an expansive landscape planted with more than seven thousand new trees, Glenstone has constructed an underground system of concrete cisterns for water storage. The largest is sited downhill from the Pavilions in order to capture runoff from the building, and has the capacity to hold 650,000 gallons of water. A second underground cistern, with a 250,000-gallon capacity, sits below the Environmental Center. Finally, a third structure is located directly underneath Jeff Koons's artwork *Split-Rocker*, 2000, which features more than twenty-two thousand blossoming plants. In season, *Split-Rocker* is watered with a drip-irrigation system; any excess water drains into the cistern, which facilitates the reuse of water and nutrients to keep these flowers in bloom.

–PT

See Also:
Concrete (76–77)

Stream Restoration

Trees

Irrigation

In an ideal world, nature would provide all the water needed for its trees, shrubs, native plants, lawn grasses, and flowers to flourish. In the real world, especially in the unpredictable mid-Atlantic region, rain flow amounts can vary significantly. As a safeguard, Glenstone has installed hundreds of miles of tubes, both above- and belowground, to bring water to its plants. Jeff Koons's *Split-Rocker*, 2000, is watered via an elaborate internal network of drip-irrigation tubes, which thread through the 240 stainless-steel boxes that form the sculpture's structural frame. Glenstone constantly monitors the moisture content of all soils to conserve as much water as possible, only supplying additional irrigation when and where needed.

–PT

See Also:
Stainless steel (86)
Sustainability (71)

Among the unique features of Glenstone's landscape is the intersection—known as a confluence—of two tributaries to the Potomac River—the Sandy Branch stream to the west and the Greenbriar Branch stream to the east. These tributaries had decayed and destabilized, containing poor water quality for fish and insects, and presenting a safety concern for visitors. To address these concerns, Glenstone contracted Dr. David Rosgen, the world's leading expert in stream and river restoration. Based on his action plan utilizing all natural materials including logs and boulders from the site, a large-scale stream restoration program began on the property in 2015. This construction is resulting in reduced sediment reaching the Potomac River, improved water quality, and a revived wildlife habitat for aquatic organisms. The stream valleys are now some of the most beautiful areas of the Glenstone landscape.

–PT

See Also:
Community (85)
Ecosystem (99)

American Sycamore
Platanus occidentalis

The American sycamore (*Platanus occidentalis*) is one of the tallest trees found in eastern North America, and has a special place in the Glenstone story. The specimen, the largest on the site, was moved in 2009 to make way for the planned Glenstone expansion, and now welcomes visitors soon after they cross the arrival bridge. Its pruning and placement were conceived to frame visitors' first view of the Pavilions. This tree has become an important touchstone for the institution, beloved by staff and a reminder of Glenstone's commitment to preserving the landscape. The sycamore's wide branches bud in spring with leaves measuring four to eight inches in diameter; in full flower, the sycamore exceeds seventy-five feet in width.

–EL

See Also:
Entrance (78)
Integration (43)
Meadow (103)
Pavilions, the (83)
Sight line (105)

American sycamore

Clockwise from top:
eastern redbud (*Cercis canadensis*), red maple (*Acer rubrum*), overcup oak (*Quercus lyrata*),
London plane (*Platanus x Acerifolia*), flowering crabapple (*Malus* 'Adams'), honey locust (*Gleditsia triacanthos*), eastern flowering dogwood (*Cornus florida*)

Clockwise from top:
southern red oak (*Quercus falcata*), white oak (*Quercus alba*), white pine (*Pinus strobus*),
tulip-tree (*Liriodendron tulipferia*), river's purple European beech (*Fagus sylvatica* 'Riversii'),
river birch (*Betula nigra*), red oak (*Quercus rubra*)

Understories

Little Bluestem
Schizachyrium scoparium

A perennial grass native to much of North America, including Maryland, little bluestem is often found in prairies and meadows. Preferring slopes and ridges, this upright, clumping grass can reach a height of three feet, with a broad range of varieties typically exhibiting a kaleidoscope of colors, from blue-green at the base to purplish-bronze at the tip, and wispy silver flowers in late summer. Highly beneficial to wildlife, especially birds, for its prodigious seed production, little bluestem is also a host plant for our native dusky skipper and common wood-nymph butterfly larvae. Its adaptability to a wide range of soils, resistance to deer, tolerance for drought, and generous root depth make it an excellent choice for prairie and meadow restoration, as well as for erosion control. In the spirit of Glenstone's vision for sustainability, little bluestem has been selected as a primary focal point of the meadows and landscape surrounding the Gallery and the Pavilions.

–MR

See Also:
Meadow (103)
Serra, Richard (64)
Soil (105–106)
Wildlife (114–115)

Clockwise from top:
dwarf fothergilla (*Fothergilla gardenii*), fescue (*Festuca brevipila*),
foxtail barley (*Hordeum jubatum*), hay-scented fern (*Dennstaedtia punctilobula*),
paw paw (*Asimina triloba*), Pennsylvania sedge (*Carex pansylvanica*),
pink muhlygrass (*Muhlenbergia capillaris*), purpletop (*Tridens flava*),
winterberry (*Ilex verticillata*)

Wildlife

Red Fox
Vulpes vulpes

The red fox (*Vulpes vulpes*) is found all over the world, and despite its name can be golden, reddish-brown, silver, or even black. The red fox typically hunts small game like rodents, rabbits, and birds, though if necessary it has also been known to feed on fish, frogs, worms, fruits, and vegetables. While these foxes are skilled hunters, they are also hunted: fox hunting as sport dates from the 1700s in England, and fox chasing—where the fox is pursued by hounds, but not killed—is still practiced in the United States. From the 1930s to the 1980s, members of the Potomac Hunt Club hunted fox on and around the land that now forms Glenstone's grounds. Though the club eventually moved north, red foxes remain frequent callers to Glenstone, with occasional sightings by visitors and staff.

–CD

See Also:
Ecosystem (99)
Meadow (103)
Pond (104)
Woodlands (116)

Clockwise, from top left:
big brown bat (*Eptesicus fuscus*), white-tailed deer (*Odocoileus virginianus*), monarch butterfly (*Danaus plexippus*), eastern pondhawk (*Erythemis simplicicollis*), lesser anglewing katydid (*Microcentrum retinerve*), ebony jewelwing (*Calopteryx maculate*), largemouth bass (*Micropterus salmoides*), spring pepper frog (*Pseudacris crucifer*), northern water snake (*Nerodia sipedon*), striped skunk (*Mephitis mephitis*), groundhog (*Marmota monax*), eastern cottontail (*Sylvilagus floridanus*)

Woodlands

Woodlands are less dense than forests, with open areas that offer sunlight without excessive shade, and can often act as transitional areas within a designed landscape. At Glenstone art and architecture work in concert with the acres of surrounding native woodlands, which are actively reforested and conserved in close collaboration with Montgomery County. Visitors can descend the stone steps behind the Gallery entrance to explore Glenstone's woodlands via a network of footpaths, where artworks installed in this secluded area can be discovered. The main Woodland Trail ends in a boardwalk, which brings visitors out of the woods to emerge into the bright and open meadow above.

—TCu

See Also:
Community (85)
Ecosystem (99)
Reforestation (105)

Index

Abstract Expressionism, 14–15
Abstraction, 14
Acid-etched glass, 80
Aeration, 106
Alaskan yellow cedar, 89
Appropriation art, 16–17
Aquatics, 94–96
Ardea herodias (Great Blue Heron), 98
Argillite, 88
Arman, 16
Arte Neoconcreta, 16
Arte Povera, 18
Asawa, Ruth, 18
Ash, 89
Assemblage, 18
Avant-garde, 19

Baer, Jo, 19
Basquiat, Jean-Michel, 19
Benglis, Lynda, 20
Beuys, Joseph, 20–21
Birds, 96–98
Bioretention areas, 107
Boetti, Alighiero e, 20
Bontecou, Lee, 22
Bourgeois, Louise, 22–23
Broodthaers, Marcel, 22

Calder, Alexander, 24–25
Camargo, Sergio, 24
Carderock, 86
Cardiff, Janet and George Bures Miller, 8–9, 26–27
Cast-in-place concrete, 76
Cistern, 107
Clark, Lygia, 26
Clerestory, 82

Climate control, 76
Collage, 26
Collection, 28
Commission, 28
Community, 85
Compost tea, 106
Conceptual art, 28–29
Concrete, 76–77
Conservation, 30–31
Contemporary art, 30

de Kooning, Willem, 32
Design, 49
Direct engagement, 35
Douglas fir, 89
Drawing, 32–33
Duchamp, Marcel, 32

Ecosystem, 99
Entrance, 78
Environmental Center, 8–9, 99
Exhibition, 34

Farm and forage, 99
Flavin, Dan, 34
Flowers, 100–102
Fluxus, 34
Forest bathing, 103
Framed views, 78–79

Gallery, the, 8–9, 78
Giacometti, Alberto, 36
Glass, 80
Gober, Robert, 8–9, 36
Goldsworthy, Andy, 8–9, 36–37
Gonzalez-Torres, Felix, 8–9, 38

Gorky, Arshile, 38
Granite, 88
Green Roof, 80
Gutai, 39
Gwathmey, Charles, 81

Hammons, David, 39
Haring, Keith, 39
Heizer, Michael, 8–9, 40
Hesse, Eva, 40–41
Hickory, 90
Horn, Roni, 40
Horticulture, 103

Impatiens hawkeri, (New Guinea Impatiens), 102
Installation, 42
Integration, 43
Ipe, 90
Irrigation, 108

Johns, Jasper, 42
Judd, Donald, 42

Kanayama, Akira, 44
Kawara, On, 44
Kelly, Ellsworth, 8–9, 44
Kippenberger, Martin, 45
Klein, Yves, 45
Kline, Franz, 45
Koons, Jeff, 8–9, 46
Kruger, Barbara, 46
Kusama, Yayoi, 46–47

LED, 82
LEED, 81
LeWitt, Sol, 48
Light, 82–83
Louver, 82

Maple, 90
Marden, Brice, 48
Martin, Agnes, 50–51
Meadow, 103
Merz, Marisa, 50
Minimal art, 50
Modern art, 52–53
Mosaiculture, 104
Motonaga, Sadamasa, 52

Nauman, Bruce, 52
Nitrogen cycle/fixation, 106
Nouveau Réalisme, 54
Nymphaea 'Marliacea Albida' (Marliac White Water Lily), 94
Oculus, 83
Oiticica, Hélio, 54
Oldenburg, Claes, 54

Painting, 55
Pape, Lygia, 55
Pavilions, the, 8–9, 83
Peter Walker and Partners, 104
Phifer, Thomas, 84
Photography, 55
Plaster, 84
Platanus occidentalis (American Sycamore), 108–109
Polke, Sigmar, 56
Pollock, Jackson, 56–57
Pond, 8–9, 104
Pop art, 56
Post-Minimal art, 58
Postmodern art, 58
Postwar art, 58
Precast concrete, 76

Printmaking, 59
Process art, 59
Public art, 60
Puryear, Martin, 60–61

Rauschenberg, Robert, 60
Ray, Charles, 62
Readymade, 62–63
Reforestation, 105
Rist, Pipilotti, 64
Roth, Dieter, 64
Rothko, Mark, 64

Schendel, Mira, 65
Schizachyrium scoparium, (Little Bluestem), 112
Sculpture, 65
Serra, Richard, 8–9, 65
Shade, 83
Shimamoto, Shozo, 66
Shiraga, Kazuo, 66–67
Sight line, 105
Site-specific, 66
Smith, Tony, 8–9, 68
Soil, 105–106
Sound art, 68
Stainless steel, 86
Stella, Frank, 68
Still, Clyfford, 69
Stone, 86–88
Storm-water management, 107–108
Stream restoration, 108
Sustainability, 71

Tanaka, Atsuko, 69
Teak, 91
Terrazzo, 88
Time-based media, 69

Tinguely, Jean, 70
Transparent glass, 80
Trees, 108–111
Trockel, Rosemarie, 70
Truitt, Anne, 70
Twombly, Cy, 72

Understories, 112–113

Vulpes vulpes (Red Fox), 114

Warhol, Andy, 72
Water Court, 88
Weiner, Lawrence, 72–73
Wildlife, 114–115
Wood, 89–91
Woodlands, 116
Yoshida, Toshio, 74

Zinc, 91

Notes

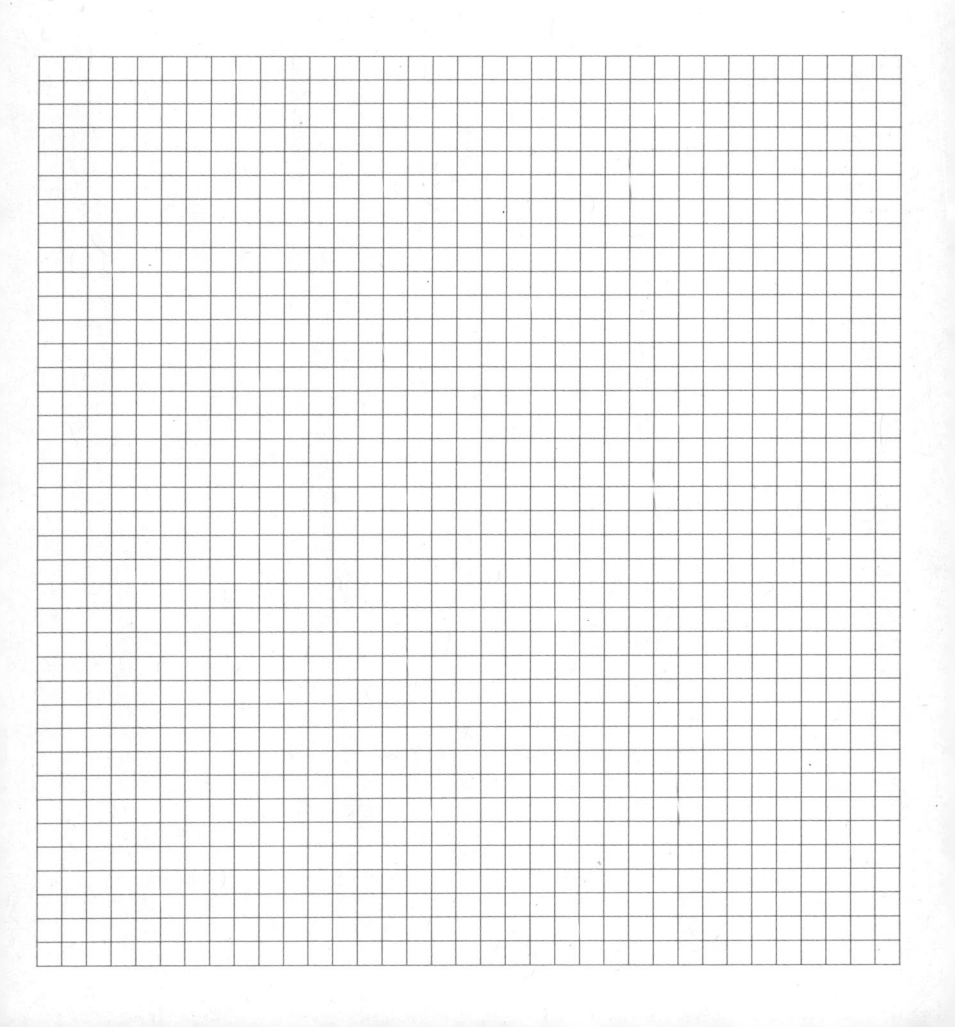

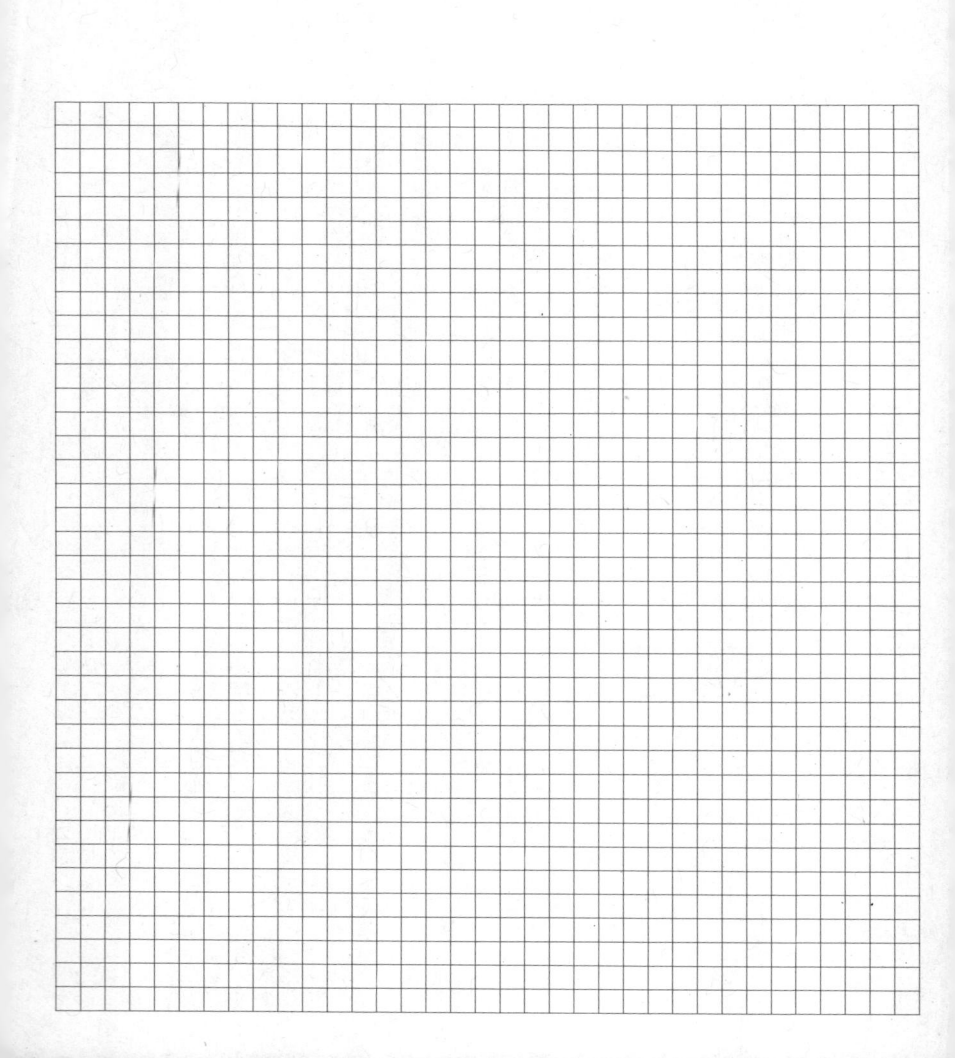

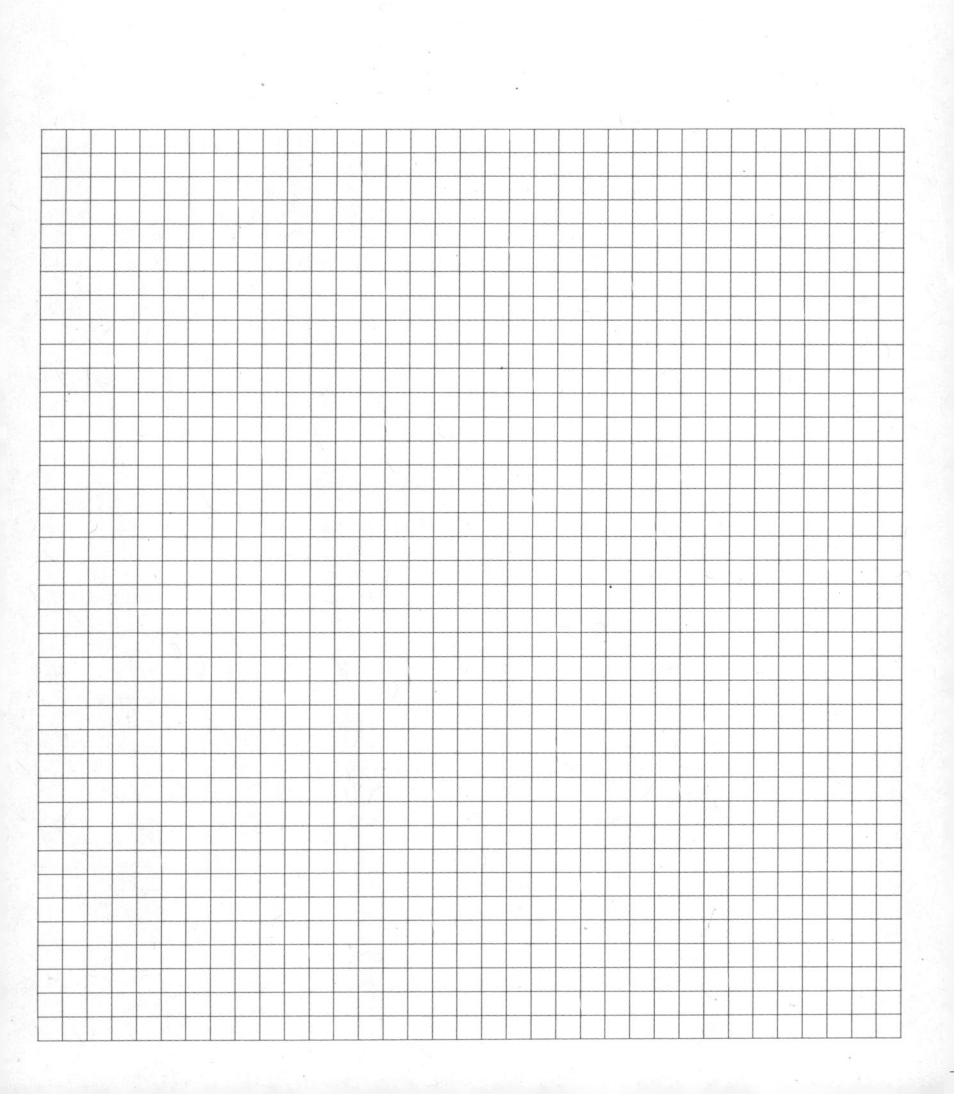

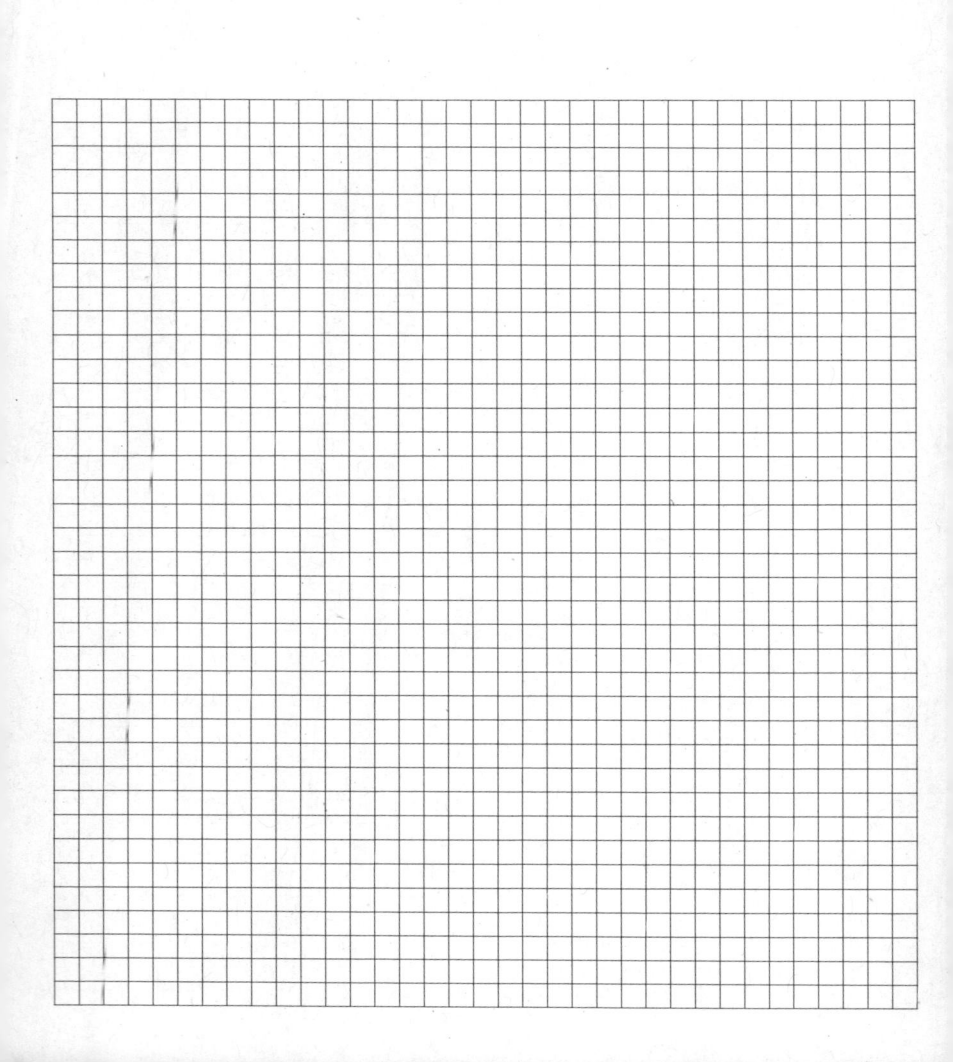

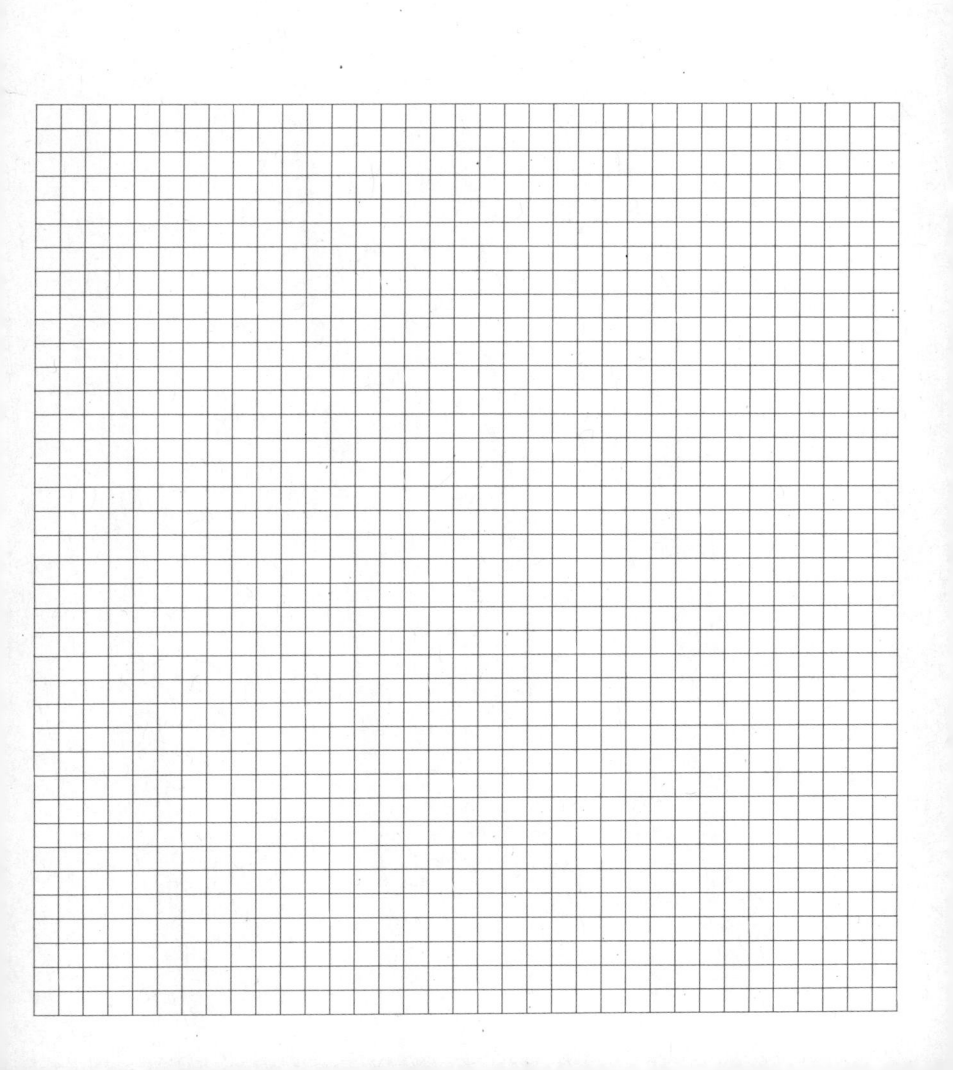

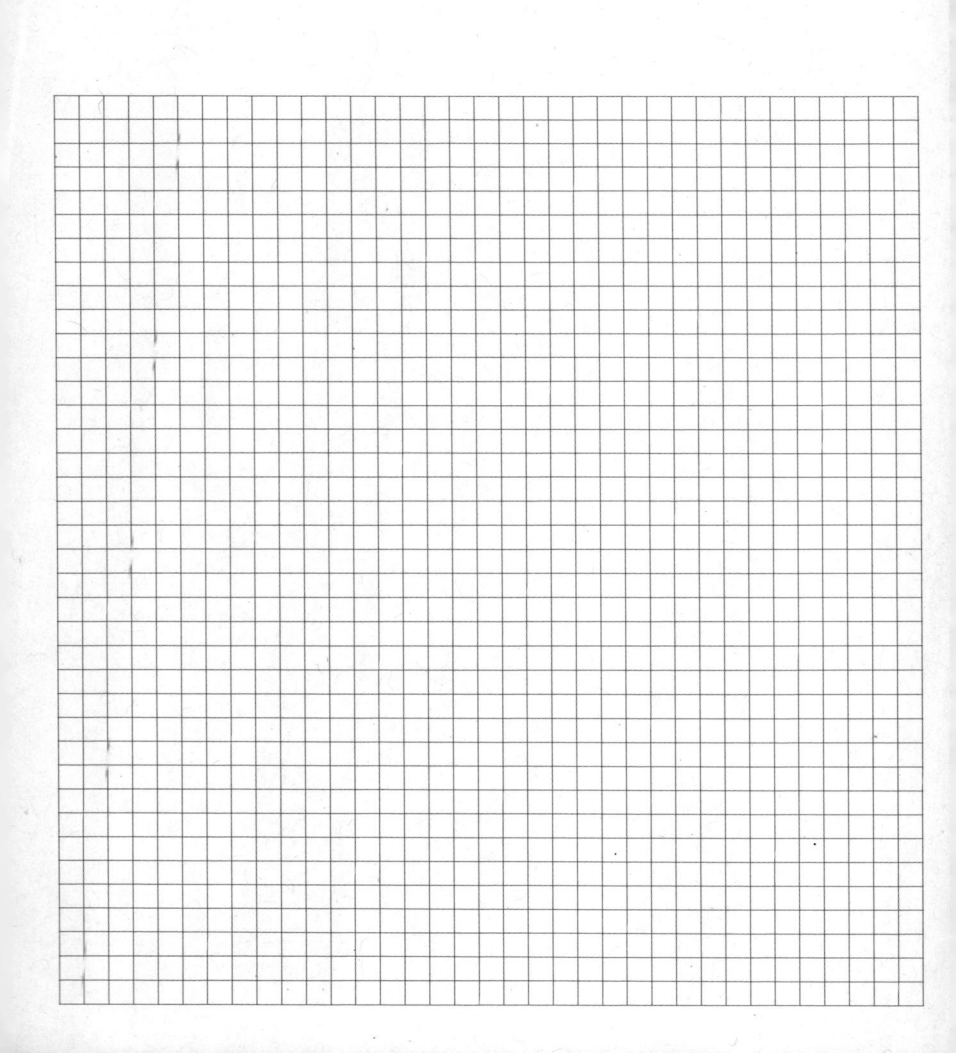

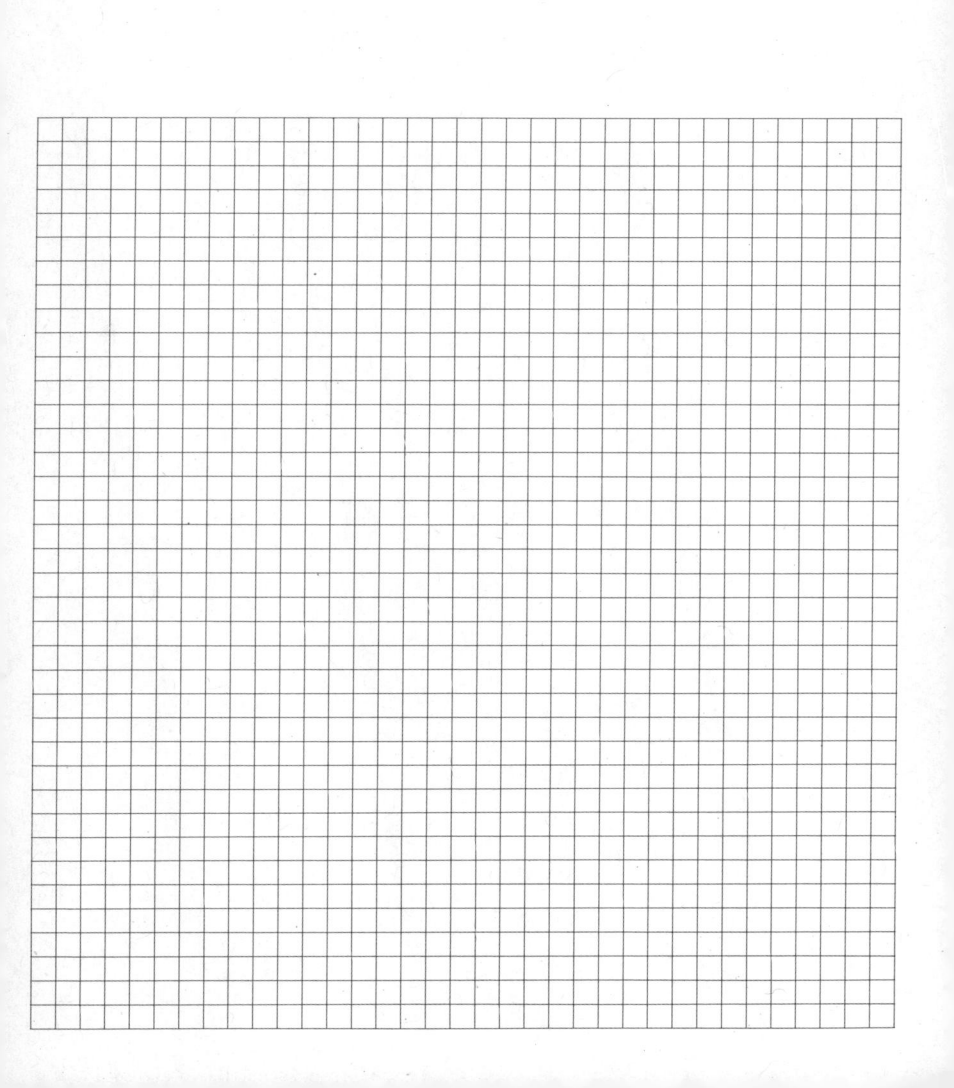

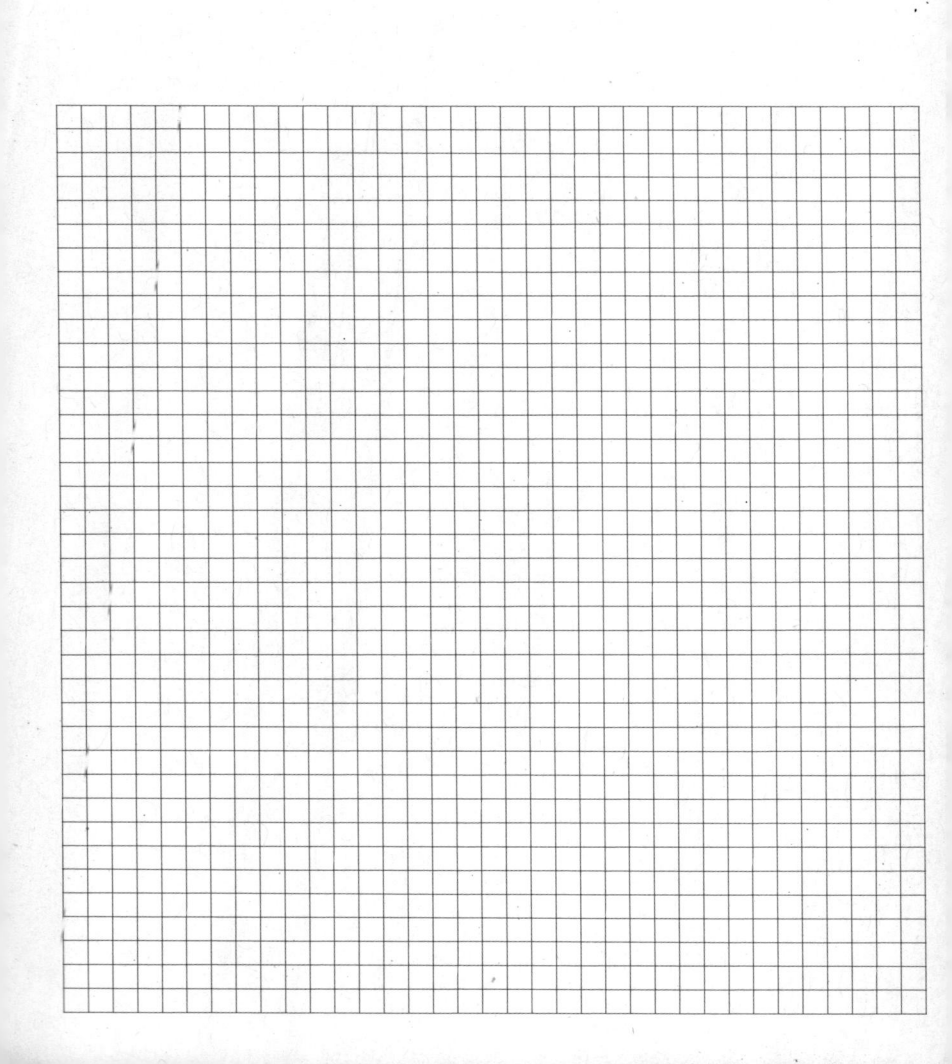

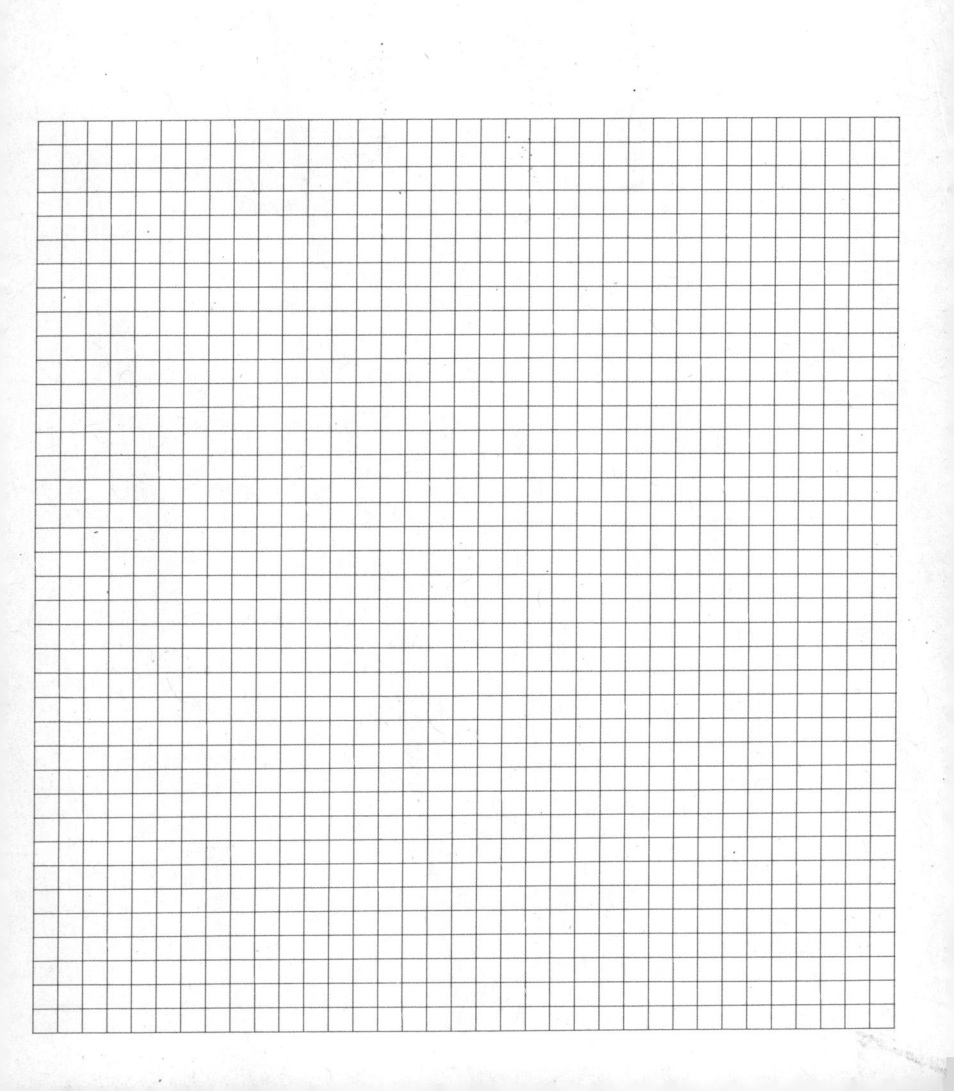

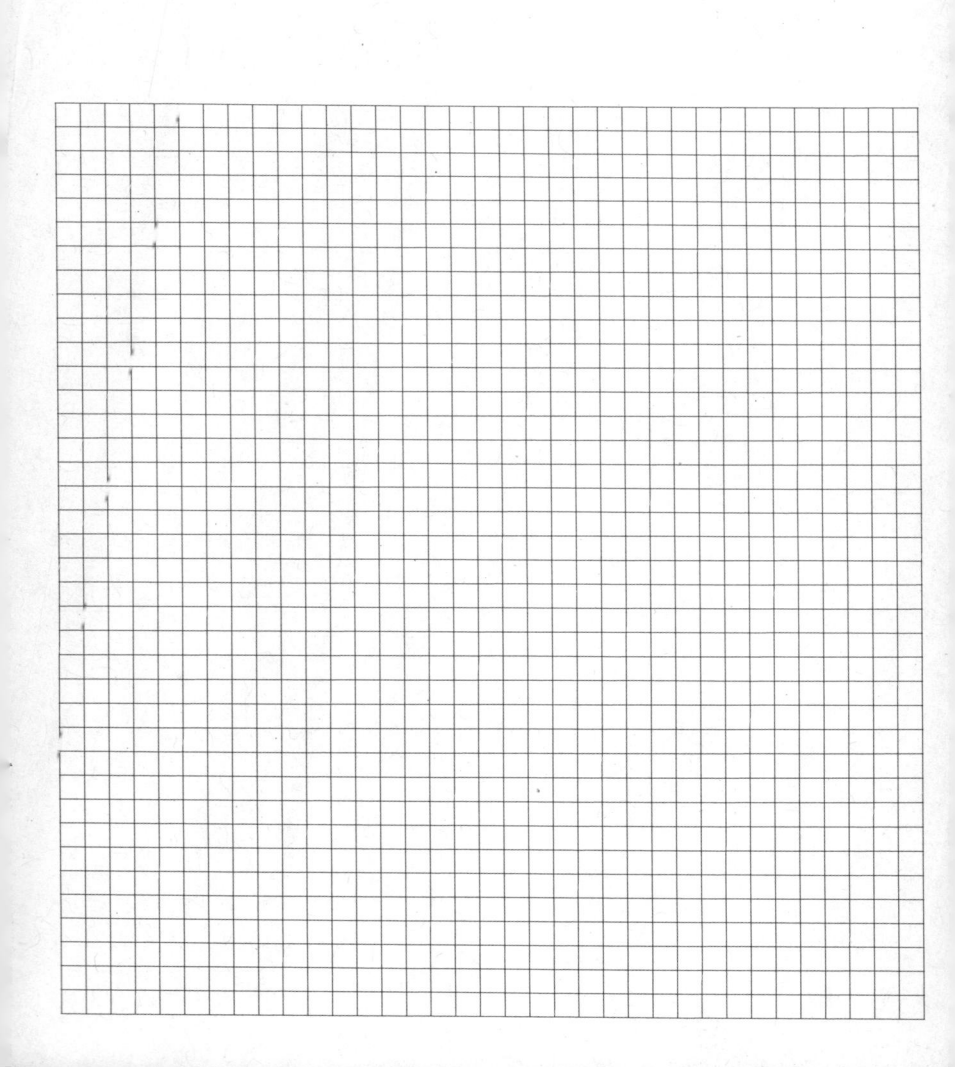